Christian Mentoring

Helping Each Other Find Meaning and Purpose

Thomas G. Bandy

Christian Mentoring
Helping Each Other Find Meaning and Purpose

(c) 2011 by Thomas G. Bandy

 BandyBooks

BV5053 BAN

Other Books by Tom Bandy:

Abingdon Press

Kicking Habits: Welcome a Relief for Addicted Churches
Growing Spiritual Redwoods (with Bill Easum)
Moving Off the Map: A Field Guide to Changing the Congregation
Christian Chaos: Revolutionizing the Congregation
Coaching Change: Breaking Down Resistance, Building Up Hope
Roadrunner: The Body in Motion
Fragile Hope: Your Church in 2020
Mission Mover: Beyond Education for Church Leadership
Uncommon Lectionary: Opening the Bible for Seekers and Disciples
Why Should I Believe You? The Crisis of Clergy Credibility
95 Questions to Shape the Future of Your Church

Chalice Press

Talisman: Global Positioning for the Soul
Christian OptiMystics (with Dwayne Ratzlaff)
Spirited Leadership: Empowering People to Do What Matters
Jesus the Christ

MissionInsite www.MissionInsite.com

Accelerate Your Church: Out of the Box and Beyond
Mission Impact: Ministry Applications for Lifestyle Portraits

Contents

A Practical Guide to Christian Mentoring

Introduction

The goal of mentoring is to shape integrity and focus vocation. The goal of explicitly Christian mentoring is to help individuals align their lifestyles and purposes for living with the model and commission of Jesus Christ.

The roots of Christian mentoring go back to Jesus himself, who selected twelve disciples and invested significant time and energy to help them align their lives to the ethic of God's love and to the purpose of God's redemption of the world.

These twelve became apostles after the resurrection, and they continued the practice of mentoring. We see many references in scripture to the selective mentoring process as Peter invested time and energy in deacons like Stephen; or as Paul invested time and energy in Timothy, Silas, Luke, and Onesimus; or as Priscilla and Aquilla invested time and energy in Apollos. There is little record in the New Testament of educational programming, although certainly churches had it. There are only scattered indications of worship liturgy, although certainly churches did that also — probably in different methods for different cultures. What is evident in the New Testament is that veteran leaders connected with chosen emerging leaders in special ways, using the relationship as a vehicle to align lifestyle and define purpose.

Apostolic succession is one, rather institutionalized way of describing the larger role of Christian mentoring in the growing church. It was so successful that today epistles in and beyond the New Testament were attributed to an original apostle. The academic debate today over the authorship of some epistles was quite irrelevant to pre-modern Christians because mentoring was the pervasive methodology of personal and spiritual growth. Individuality and originality were things to be avoided. Faithful recollection and application of eternal truths and profound wisdom were prized. What did it matter if the real author of Galatians was not Paul? It was written by one mentored by Paul, as if it were actually written by Paul, and Paul's authorship was as "real" as if he himself had inscribed the words.

Mentoring of any kind has almost become a lost methodology in the modern world. Individualism and originality became higher values than community and obedience. Life became too mobile, frantic, and demanding to allow much time to be invested in companionship with a few disciples and other emerging leaders. The modern world created "shortcuts" for education by funneling people through age-based programs in public schools, topical curricula for carefully channeled university degrees, and professional training tailored to the needs of public consumption and dysfunction. If educators prioritized too much time to mentor a few promising students, the institution complained that their classes were too small.

Christian mentoring has also waned as the church accommodated to modern culture. Church institutions created similar "shortcuts" for education by funneling people through Sunday schools, confirmation classes, and theological curricula ... as if a book, video, or digital slide show could replace a relationship as a discipline of accountability, or an intentional and ongoing conversation. The institutional church trained clergy to construct sermons, manage programs, maintain budgets, and counsel those suffering from grief or illness, but not to mentor Christians. If clergy did prioritize time and energy to mentor twelve disciples, the church complained to the Bishop that (s)he wasn't visiting enough.

The decline of mentoring in the modern era, and the recovery of mentoring in the post-modern era, is closely tied to our shifting notions of "truth" and "verifiability." Wisdom has traditionally been associated with the alignment of our hearts with the universal mysteries of goodness, beauty, and truth. Mentoring has been the primary method of communicating "heart to heart" so that individuals can judiciously find their way through the ambiguities of daily living, model goodness, beauty, and truth to the best of their ability, and eventually find personal fulfillment through participation in a higher purpose.

Modernity changed all that. Truth became information, reduced to rationalized, manipulated data bytes. Beauty became emotion, reduced to self-centered, passionate aggressiveness. Goodness became perspective, reduced to one among many political options. What people analyzed became more important than what they synthesized. What "I" felt became more important than what "thou" felt. What a person did became more important than who a person was. Mentoring does not readily translate into quantifiable increases in influence, independence, and income. It does connect with qualitative experiences of justice, love, and meaning. These are the very things post-modern people yearn to rediscover. The modern reductions of truth, and years of merely professional education, have made skepticism and cynicism the new religious dogmatisms of our age. More and more post-modern people are ready to risk the inquisition, believing that there has got to be more to education than this.

Mentoring is decidedly counter-cultural, often mysterious, and needlessly complicated from the perspective of modern culture. Perhaps that is why post-modern culture seeks mentoring so earnestly, or perhaps it is this intuition about the limitations of modern education and the desire for mentoring that has precipitated the post-modern world. Post-moderns look to pre-moderns to understand what mentoring is really all about.

First, mentoring is all about *experience* ... not expertise. Mentors speak from the "school of hard knocks" and from the "school of hard-fought victories" that have occurred in their personal lives. This is one reason why the ancients (and eastern and Native American cultures) have revered older people. However, in our world, young people have often experienced a lifetime of pain and hope in just a few short years, and it is entirely possible that young people may be able to speak from experience even more powerfully than seniors.

Mentoring is not really about expertise. One does not have to have professional training in therapy or advanced degrees in any particular subject. Expertise may be helpful in particular situations and mentors frequently seek continuing education in order to bond, communicate, or advise unique individuals facing specific challenges. Yet it is the experience of coping with life and discerning hope that is more important.

Second, mentoring is all about *insight* ... not information. Mentors synthesize information, and make intuitive leaps beyond the data to discern root causes and underlying assumptions. They "see" the hidden potential in people and events, or the self-destructive habits and recurring themes behind behavior. They are keen observers who are never quite sure what they are looking for ... until they see it.

Mentoring is not really about mastering, sorting, or analyzing data. Taking things apart and putting them back together misses the point. Human beings are always more than their constituent biological systems or psychological states. Mentors are convinced that human beings have a "soul" ... that the soul can be simultaneously shaped by choice and providence ... and that insight into the soul of another is a form of revelation. Analysis is content with reality. Insight searches for truth that lies behind, or beyond, reality.

Third, mentoring is all about *wisdom* ... not explanation. Mentors sharply distinguish between *why* and *how*. They explore motivation and purposefulness,

Mentoring is about ...

✓ **experience, not expertise;**
✓ **insight, not information;**
✓ **wisdom, not explanation;**
✓ **self-discipline, not disciplines; and**
✓ **surrender, not self.**

which together form the *intentionality* that the individual brings to living. Mentors help seekers adjust to the mystery of gratuitous evil and unexpected miracle, maintaining a sense of direction in the midst of ambiguity.

Mentoring is not really about rationalizations that explain away mysteries as logical sequences of events. Pat answers, repetitive dogmas, aphorisms, and moralizations are foreign to the mentor. No conversation is ever quite finished; no explanation is ever quite sufficient; no perspective is ever quite complete. There is a truth, but it cannot be contained in words. An individual life can align with truth without ever fully grasping it.

Fourth, mentoring is all about *self-discipline* ... not academic disciplines. Mentors demonstrate how to lead an ordered life. They control their passions, proceed judiciously in their actions, practice spiritual habits, exercise body and mind, and take responsibility for relationships. Self-discipline allows them to channel their energy in targeted directions of attention. They are not easily distracted by personal needs and problems, and can focus on the other.

Mentoring is not really about academic disciplines. Every field of study has its own procedures about work, but demands much less rigor for the lifestyle of the worker. The most careful researchers can live the most careless lives. The most learned teachers can be the most eccentric and amoral individuals. So long as you perform well, you can live as you like.

Finally, mentoring is all about surrender ... not self. Mentors move beyond self-discipline to self-forgetfulness. They try to "get out of themselves" so that they can better understand the seeker ... or better immerse themselves in truth. The ego gets in their way, which is why they try so hard to tame it and get beyond it. Their humility is part of their credibility.

Mentoring is not really about self-actualization, personal creativity, or unleashing individuality. This is very difficult to understand, especially in modern western culture. Starting with the renaissance and extending through the enlightenment, modern western people have defined the ego ... the individual ... as the center of the universe. It is simply incomprehensible that anyone might deny personal survival, individual accomplishment, or private satisfaction as the ultimate motivations and goals of living. Mentors do. Therefore, modern western people have consistently preferred teachers. Teachers help you take control of the aspects of your life (career, marriage, family, leisure). Mentors help you stake all that for a higher purpose.

What makes mentoring explicitly Christian is that the experience, model, commission, and companionship of Jesus Christ are central. Mentors generally believe that beyond all personal perspectives, there are absolutes that can be pursued and, in some approximation, achieved. These may be classical Platonic ideals of love, beauty, honor, or truth, but they may also be ideological agendas, ladders of success, or ecstasies of personal satisfaction. Behind all the skepticism of modernity, there lies a hidden conviction that somehow, somewhere, "the truth is out there!"

A similar state of skepticism and yearning existed in the early centuries of the Roman Empire. Various philosophies competed with the stoicism epitomized by Marcus Aurelius, along variations of capitalism and socialism, mystical cults, and extraordinary hedonism. Christian faith represented a dramatic, distinct alternative to these competing philosophies because the truth was not only "out there" but also "down here" ... and at one and the same time.

Today it is the experience of incarnation that sparks the recovery of ancient methods of mentoring. So long as goodness, beauty, and truth remain unreachably "out there," the *best* we can achieve will be dreamy skepticism. The burgeoning media industries for fantasy, romance, and science fiction are today the primary outlets for career professionals and day laborers who dream of something more. But if goodness, beauty, and truth were suddenly, unexpectedly, "down here" everything would change. There would still be a divine mystery, but that mystery would suddenly be *accessible*. It could be explored. More importantly, it could make a difference. It could change the world, and the world could no longer safely hide behind an impregnable wall of skepticism. Socrates helped his disciples die nobly. Jesus helped his disciples live abundantly.

Me? Mentor? Maybe?

The Christian experience significantly broadens the potential of mentoring. More people have access to mentoring. Not only can the wealthy, educated, cultured, and privileged classes of society reasonably hope to find mentors that can shape their lives and guide them toward their destinies. Now the poor, uneducated, vulgar, and underprivileged can hope for the same. Similarly, more people are called to become mentors. Not only can professional, intellectual, certified, and salaried people legitimately mentor seekers toward abundant life. Now amateur, illiterate, unsophisticated, and unpaid volunteers can do the same. Christianity's unique experience of incarnation universalized access to mentoring … but it also raised the standard of accountability for Christians to take responsibility for mentoring.

One reason that Christianity was a scandal to the gentiles was that it broke down class distinctions. The basic view of Christian mentoring is revealed in the New Testament.

Every human being is gifted … blessed by God with personality traits and unique talents. Certain attitudes and behavior patterns seem natural, and other attitudes and behavior patterns seem foreign. Certain skills come easily, and other skills seem difficult to acquire. This does not mean that people cannot change. It simply means that individuals are "wired" differently. If individuals choose to do so, they can alter their personalities and acquire new skills through therapy or education.

Every Christian is called … transformed by God into a "new creation," obedient to a "new Master," and called to follow the way of Christ. The Christian "way" is different than the "ways of the world" … sometimes complementary, sometimes contradictory, and sometimes simply indifferent. The Christian "way" is both a journey and a destination. It is a road leading to a particular place. Christ is on the road with us. Christ is at the end of the road to receive us. It is important that Christians behave "on the road" in a manner that imitates the ethic and attitude of Jesus, because only in so doing can they arrive at the "end of the road" to be in ultimate unity with Christ.

Some Christians are called *to be mentors* for other Christians. These are leaders who are further "down the road" than other Christians, but deliberately "double back" to walk with less mature Christians who are journeying behind them. Their companionship and conversation helps "younger" Christians adopt the ethic and attitude of Jesus. They are there to encourage and reprove, evoking the best from the hearts of believers, and sometimes provoking them to work harder, walk faster, or serve better. Most of all, they are there to prevent sidetracks, urging Christians on the "way" to endure and persist, maintaining a straight course toward joyful unity with Christ. Don't wander, don't misbehave, don't hinder the journeys of others, and don't stop. Go straight, model the ethic of Jesus, help others mature, and keep going.

Modern Christians typically doubt that they might be called to be mentors. Given modern understandings of education, this is not surprising. We equate teachers with experts, and expect them to be professionals. Anyone who aspires to be a "mentor" must therefore be a saint ... or at least a veteran professional who is certifiably holy. This places an unsupportable burden on a few paid staff, and while their egos may get a boost, inwardly they quake in their boots. They know that they were never equipped to do anything like mentoring, and that if they did it the wider congregation would complain for lack of pastoral counseling and sound financial management. The modern attitude also allows church members to escape accountability through a sense of false humility. *I couldn't possibly do that! I would seem arrogant if I tried!* If one cannot be expert, then surely one must be inactive.

The Holy Spirit, however, will just not leave us alone. Many may avoid responsibility to mentor others in the Christian journey, but some (more than you think!) are inwardly pondering a higher calling. They are restless people. They are convinced there has to be more to Christian life than going to church and percentage giving. They have the audacity to take their baptismal vows seriously. The more they ponder the incarnation, the more restless they become. What good is the "Good News" unless you pass it on?

Are you a potential mentor? There are seven indicators that you may be among the chosen ... or perhaps it is better to say "the driven." Being a mentor is often not something you choose to do. It is something into which you are precipitated by the Holy Spirit whether you like it or not. If you ask mentors how they started mentoring, they are likely to say that they simply found themselves mentoring others. There was no actual point when they started. They just realized that was what they were doing.

So these seven indicators are used to confirm what you already find yourself doing. One day you realize that people are coming to you for guidance. Church members, seekers, skeptics, and even people angry at religion ... business associates, neighbors, family relations, and even strangers ... they all seem to be sharing confidences, looking for leadership, hoping for meaning, and dragging you into their disastrous or uncomfortable living because *somehow* they think you can help them realize hidden hopes.

That realization scares many people to death. "Who, me? How do I dare? Am I presumptuous? Will I do more harm than good?" So use these seven indicators as a way to reflect on your purpose, confirm your calling, and perhaps identify your strengths and weaknesses as a mentor.

1. Consciousness of having received mentoring
   (People in various times and places, intentional and unintentional, who shaped your life)

2. Memories of past, personal experiences of the Holy
   (Experiences with God as promise-keeper, healer, guide, vindicator, model, and higher power)

3. Participatory experience in a system of accountability
   (Accountability for attitude, integrity, skills/competency, and teamwork in any sector of living)

4. Personal victories in the midst of universal anxieties
   (Universal anxieties such as emptiness and meaninglessness, fate and death, guilt and condemnation)

5. Humility before the mystery of incarnation
   (Feelings of awe, awareness of personal limitations, readiness to learn, and need for confession)

6. Compulsion for the redemptive purpose of God
   (Desire to be a part of God's unfolding salvation history)

7. Recognition that you are already a mentor
   (For better or worse, you are a "parent" who is already a role model for others)

All good mentors seek mentoring from others. Use the same seven indicators to look for someone to be your own mentor.

1) Consciousness of Having Received Mentoring

Mentors have themselves experienced mentoring. Look back on the course of your life — especially on times of transition. You may not have consciously thought about it before, but certain individuals stand out as influential, even crucial, to your progress. These relationships may have been deliberately formed, coincidental in the midst of doing something else, or entirely unplanned and unexpected. Yet they deepened, redirected, or transformed your life.

Consider first your family relationships. Often individuals who did *not* have direct responsibility for your financial support (i.e. parents) have the most impact in shaping your life: brothers, sisters, grandparents, aunts or uncles, cousins, etc. Such people take a deliberate and self-sacrificial interest in your lifestyle, career, life goals, and overall success as a human being.

Second, consider your personal growth relationships. In the long list of teachers, professors, doctors, pastors, and social workers that have passed through your life, certain individuals stand out. You can still see their faces, recall the timbre of their voices, quote important comments, or remember sharing certain activities. Such people went beyond imparting information and impersonal advice to "take you under their wing" and give you special attention. They saw some hidden potential in you and tried to help you give birth to a new perspective.

Next, consider your business associates and career networks. We all remember how difficult it can be to adjust to a new job, a new office, a new shift, or a new crew. In the midst of all the competitive and suspicious behavior, however, certain individuals sometimes stood out. They had the confidence to befriend you. They "showed you the ropes," gave you tips, and shared sandwiches from their own lunch boxes. In the more "white collar" world, they adopted you as a protégé, and guided you through the complexities of work and the stresses of management.

Next, consider your friends. You have probably moved in and out of peer groups all your life, but certain friends have kept up with you wherever you went. They are there for you in times of sorrow and joy. They are ready with personal support and they are constant cheerleaders in your life. They advised you in the major transition points of your life … changing jobs, falling in and out of love, overcoming disease, or relocating to another city. If you lose touch with these friends, and then unexpectedly reconnect, you are instantly bonded again.

Don't forget strangers. Mentors may have emerged in your life in unlikely places. The mentoring that lasted only a few moments at the airport, waiting in a long queue, or on a park bench, may have had an extraordinary impact on the direction of your life. You might later strain to remember the name of the person, but the experience is forever. One reason why scripture encourages you to welcome strangers is that you might find yourself entertaining angels in disguise.

Are you conscious of having received mentoring? Ponder what these mentors said and how they behaved. What did they reveal in word and deed? How did they help elicit hidden potential from within you … and how did they help challenge you to confront sidetracks, addictions, and obstacles? How were you different because of this? Your attitudes, behavior patterns, plans, and life goals were reshaped or redirected. Knowing from personal experience how mentors mentor may be an indication of your own call to mentoring.

Notice that I have not mentioned spouses in the context of remembering mentors. This is not because a husband or wife doesn't have enormous influence on your life. Their influence, however, is often nuanced by many layers of emotional, psychological, and sexual overtones. There are complex physical, financial, and family obligations. In a husband-wife relationship, the objectivity required in true mentoring is often hard to achieve. A spouse may find it difficult to intentionally evoke your hidden potential, and provoke your awareness of obstacles, because they have such a personal "stake" in your old habits and predictable lifestyle. This is why spouses may find it difficult to be mentors to the very people they love the most.

Nevertheless, there are stages in married life when a spouse can be a mentor. You may remember times when your life was in a particularly stressful transition. Perhaps it involved a change of career, a crisis of health, or an unexpected grief. Sometimes spouses can distance themselves from their personal stake in your behavior, and with compassionate objectivity help you reach new levels of self-understanding or purpose. As we shall see, spousal intimacy can point toward a second indication that you might be called to mentoring.

2) Memories of Past, Personal Experiences of the Holy

Mentors always have mystical memories of times when they felt the awesome presence of God. Some of these experiences are beyond words. Mentors may tell stories, draw pictures, or create music as the only means to communicate them. They may also simply be struck dumb and remain silent. Some of these experiences, however, can be set to words. The mentor will try to share them, explain them, and communicate them to any who have "ears to hear and eyes to see."[1]

Think back on your own life. Have you experienced mystical moments when you felt God close to you? Many modern people have difficulty recovering these experiences, because the contemporary culture of rationalization has led them to "explain them away" in a spirit of skepticism. Interpreting certain experiences as "God moments" seems childish, immature, and even crazy. However, you may be one of an increasing number of modern people who are beginning to be skeptical of the skepticism. You may wonder if there really wasn't something more in the experience … some intersection with the supernatural … some connection with a High Power.

As you examine your personal "history with the Holy," it is important that you separate the "sentimental" from the "profound." Here are some guidelines that you can use to test your memories of the Holy.

- *A sense of awe*

    Authentic experiences of the Holy impress you with a deep respect for the almighty God. You experience profound humility. You feel very small and insignificant, and therefore enormously blessed and loved, simultaneously. You are compelled to surrender to a higher purpose that is beyond yourself and your immediate relationships.

- *A feeling of nobility*

    Authentic experiences of the Holy raise your self esteem. It is not that you feel like you *deserve* to be blessed, but that by being blessed you can become a blessing to others. God's presence

---

[1] I share case studies and experiences of the Holy in my book *Talisman: Global Positioning for the Soul* (St. Louis: Chalice Press, 2006).

"ennobles" you, and you feel that you are a part of salvation history. You are an ordinary vessel that God has filled with riches.

- *A sense of urgency*

  Authentic experiences of the Holy make you eager ... earnest ... about sharing the riches of God with others. You do not keep it to yourself — you are filled with a desire to share with others. Such experiences are timeless, but they result in a desperate awareness of the shortness of time. You become impatient to take action, share hope, do things that benefit others.

- *A readiness to risk*

  Authentic experiences of the Holy make you reckless. You want to "throw caution to the wind" and are ready to go beyond your comfort zones. You are prepared to look foolish and make mistakes, confident that your heart is in the right place and that you can learn from failure. You are even open to experiencing some pain for the sake of the gain in living and sharing the Holy.

It has probably occurred to the reader that this method of discerning between the "sentimental" and the "profound" is exactly how people discern whether or not they are in love. *Am I in love? Or is it just a temporary infatuation? Do I really love this woman or this man ... or is it merely a sentimental attachment?* The same criteria we use to determine if we are falling in love can be used to determine if we are truly in the presence of God.

Every time we feel we are in the immediate presence of God, it feels like falling in love. All the same feelings of anxiety, fear, trepidation, and hope are there. When we fall in love with a man or woman, we feel that same sense of awe, nobility, urgency, and risk. We are thunderstruck by the beauty, personality, and perfection of the beloved. Just being near the beloved makes us feel wonderful, important, and blessed. We feel an urgent desire to be with the beloved at all times, to touch and be touched, and to be in constant communication. And we want to tell the world about our beloved and the joys of being in love. We are ready to take enormous risks for the sake of the beloved. We will change careers, relocate to different cities, change our lifestyles, and do whatever it takes to win a smile and stay close to the beloved.

Authentic experiences of the Holy are often described as the absolute perfection of love ... the relationship of lover and beloved. Our human affection is profound, but even this is but an approximation of the "perfect love" that is experienced with God. God becomes so real to us that our bodies tingle. Infinity is right there in the midst of our reality. Therefore, Christians always describe experiences of the Holy in the language of incarnation.

- *An intimacy with Christ*

    Authentic experiences of the Holy always come back to intimacy with Jesus Christ. Later we will talk about how the experience of Christ can be felt or interpreted in many ways. Christ may be experienced as healer or vindicator, spiritual guide or perfect friend, life-changing higher power or promise keeper. For Christians, the experience of the Holy is perfectly described in the face of Christ.

- *A compass for living*

    Authentic experiences of the Holy provide a purpose and direction for your life. You may not know exactly what to do at any given moment, but you always have a fixed point of reference with which to compare your current lifestyle choices. The experience of Christ keeps you "on track." You can test everything against an absolute. *Is this what Jesus would do? Is this where Jesus would go? Is this what Jesus would spend time on?*

The lover will reprioritize all aspect of life in order to "be with" the beloved. The experience of the Holy permeates our consciousness.

3) Participatory Experience in a System of Accountability

Mentors always have some experience with serious systems of accountability. They are unafraid of being held accountable. They are assertive in holding others accountable. These experiences of accountability often come from our occupational lives, and sometimes from our lives as volunteers. Most businesses hold managers, support staff, and all employees accountable to specific job descriptions, and define anticipated measurable results that are used in annual evaluations. Public schools and hospitals, for example, publicly post "core values" in various visible locations in the building so that the public can hold teachers and health care workers accountable for their behavior.

Experience in non-profit systems of accountability can be especially beneficial if you think you are called to be a mentor. These organizations understand that accountability extends to unpaid volunteers as well as paid employees. Moreover, their systems of accountability go beyond simple skills development and statistically measurable results.

Have you had experience in a *comprehensive* system of accountability? Such accountability includes not only competency and skills development but also accountability for mission attitude, behavioral integrity, and teamwork.[2]

- *Mission attitude* refers to the underlying commitment you have to the higher purpose or ultimate concern of the organization with which you work. Employees who share a mission attitude don't watch the clock, and they work hard without constant supervision. Volunteers who share a mission attitude sacrifice more time, energy, and money, and evaluate mission results. Your attitude is revealed in your readiness to learn and go beyond your comfort zones. This is a higher accountability.

- *Behavioral integrity* refers to the alignment of both your skilled labor and your lifestyle with the values and beliefs of the organization with which you work. Doctors do not abuse drugs; teachers do not behave disrespectfully to minorities; trusted managers do not gamble away their incomes in casinos. Your integrity is revealed in the unrehearsed words and spontaneous deeds that fill your time at work and at play. This is a higher accountability.

- *Teamwork* refers to your ability to be patient, cooperative, and supportive with others. Team players sacrifice ego for the sake of team success. They listen carefully, interact respectfully, treat each other sensitively, and collaborate effectively. Organizations are learning from sports, music, and other high performance experiences to maximize results. Your teamwork is revealed

---

[2] I talk about this system of accountability extensively in my book *Spirited Leadership: Empowering People to Do What Matters* (St. Louis: Chalice Press, 2007).

through your ability to overcome personality and cultural differences. This is a higher accountability.

This more comprehensive experience with accountability is particularly helpful in mentoring. While it may be more common in non-profit organizations, it is increasingly common in business. Senior managers are applying the same principles to guide large corporations. Middle managers are learning to develop workplace teams. Small business owners are learning how to hire, train, evaluate, and (if necessary) fire employees or volunteers fairly.

Surprisingly, there are more than a few people who have never had experience with such a comprehensive accountability system. These individuals may still be called to be mentors, but they will need to learn accountability for themselves in order to apply it to others. Some laborers only know how to punch a clock. Some tenured professors fall back on guarantees for employment. Some teachers only know how to communicate a curriculum. Some corporate executives only know how to measure profits. Many employees and volunteers in profit and non-profit organizations are treated simply as numbers and workers, and long to receive the personal attention of mentoring.

Also surprisingly, the modern church is often the *least likely* place where comprehensive systems of accountability are experienced. This contrasts with the actual roots of every Christian denomination. In the beginning, churches were the best models for accountability. Today, churches often misunderstand accountability to be "judgmental," and allow all kinds of small and large abuses to go unchecked. The result is loss of credibility amid the general public, and diminished effectiveness in accomplishing missions.[3]

So ... have you participated in a system of accountability? Are you afraid of being held accountable for mission attitude, high integrity, skills and competency, and teamwork? Or do you feel timid about holding others accountable for these things? If you are confident enough to be willing to be held accountable, and if you are courageous enough to hold others accountable, these are indicators that you might be ready to be a mentor.

---

[3] I discuss accountability in the context of credible church leadership in my book *Why Should I Believe You? Recovering Clergy Credibility* (Nashville: Abingdon Press, 2006).

4) Personal Victories in the Midst of Universal Anxieties

Mentors are always able to share personal victories in the midst of universally experienced anxieties. In other words, they not only empathize with the anxiety or suffering of others, but they can speak from their own experiences of survival, endurance, and hope. Mentors have "been there, done that" and found a way to move forward in personal growth. They identify with people in need, but have little patience with people who are chronically "needy." They are confident that others can be empowered to overcome difficulties, because they themselves have been able to do so. They speak from personal experience.

Of course this does not suggest that mentors will never be anxious again. Even mentors will suffer again, worry again, be afraid again, fail again, feel guilty again, and be anxious again. There may even be a time when a mentor no longer has the confidence to be a mentor ... and must instead seek mentoring. Mentors make no claim to perfection, and are not falsely confident that they will always be "OK." At this point, at this time, with this person, they are able to both empathize and advise. They are givers of hope. This hope is not abstract or theoretical. It is hope that is borne from personal experiences of life struggles and victories.

The fundamental anxieties that beset all human beings were defined well by my own mentor, Paul Tillich.[4] I elaborate on them and apply them to Christian mentoring in my own work. No one escapes these three universal anxieties, but mentors are able to describe their methods of coping and their occasional breakthroughs.

- The anxiety of emptiness and meaninglessness

  Everyone is anxious that life might be purposeless and without meaning. Everything that happens is statistically random. We are but cogs in a mechanism, or pawns on a chessboard. We are tempted to curl up in the fetal position, withdraw from society, or surrender to mere selfishness.

  Mentors are able to share their courage to participate in relationships and life. They model for others how to surrender ego to a higher purpose. They may not explain everything, but they can

---

[4] *The Courage to Be* (New Haven: Yale University Press, 1952).

underline the meaning of some experiences and events. They give people a good reason not to give up.

In Christian perspective, mentors point to the experience of Christ as a perfect model for humanity and as a spiritual guide through ambiguity. Their belief in that mystery helps them encourage others to overcome anxiety and live with confidence.

Perhaps you doubt that you could ever witness or encourage others through your personal victories over emptiness and meaninglessness. You are naturally self-effacing. But examine your life more carefully. Certainly there have been times of doubt, and there will be more times of doubt tomorrow. Yet you live. Did you find new meaning in marriage and family life? Did you find renewed purpose in social service? Did you also experience moments of abundant life and joy in critical life transitions?

- The anxiety of fate and death

Everyone is anxious that they may be doomed by genetics, economics, culture, or demonic control. And we are anxious that the hidden network of manipulation in which we fear to live leads only to death and nothing more. We are tempted to abandon hope, get drunk, or kill ourselves.

Mentors are able to share their courage to take risks, affirm their identity, rise above chaos, and take control of their lives. They may not always succeed, but they can bear witness to the possibility of changing your direction in life, confronting self-destructive habits, and wrestling victory from defeat. They can share their conviction that death is not the end … and that there is some kind of life after death.

In Christian perspective, mentors point to the experience of Christ as a "Higher Power" that gives us a fresh start, and a "Promise Keeper" that gives us hope. Their belief in that mystery helps them reassure and liberate others to become the best that they can be.

Perhaps you doubt that you could ever exhort or empower others through your personal victories over fate and death. You are naturally modest. But if you examine your life carefully, you may rediscover a greater freedom from despair and hope for tomorrow than you realize. Has a "Higher Power" ever liberated you from self-destructive behavior patterns that you chronically denied (i.e. addictions)? Have you ever overcome the death of a loved one, and rebuilt a life with joy and purpose? Have you struggled to overcome disease? Have you labored to overcome racial violence or cultural prejudice?

- The anxiety of guilt and condemnation

  Everyone is anxious that their failures and mistakes will catch up with them. We feel guilt not just for imagined deeds, but for real deeds that seem unforgivable. We know that we are more evil than we admit to others, or even to ourselves. We fear that if real justice were to prevail, we would be among the condemned that truly deserve their punishment.

  Mentors are able to share their courage to accept forgiveness. No matter how bad their past deeds, they cling to the belief that forgiveness is possible. That is the source of *true humility*. They admit how bad they really are, and their helplessness to ever "deserve" salvation, but they celebrate their own experience of being treated mercifully.

  In Christian perspective, mentors point to the experience of Christ as healer and vindicator. Their belief in that mystery helps them comfort and rehabilitate even the worst offenders. They help people "forgive others, even as they themselves have been forgiven" (Matthew 6:14).

  Perhaps you doubt that you could ever comfort or rehabilitate others. You may be forgetful of your own experiences of renewal. Have you ever behaved badly and sworn never to repeat the same mistake? Have you every hurt others deeply, and experienced their forgiveness? Have you every confessed your sins, and felt an overwhelming sense of acceptance? Have you ever used the phrase "Once I was like this ... but now I am different?"

As we shall see later, one of the goals of mentoring is to help people recall, rediscover, and celebrate their own victories over anxiety. It may be that receiving mentoring may help you clarify your abilities to help others in each category. Yet even serious reflection, meditation, and prayer can help you explore how you have fared amid the universal anxieties of life. If you are a baptized Christian, or if you regularly confess your sins and believe in the words of assurance, you have already made a beginning and are further down the road of spiritual maturity than most of the general public.

5) Humility before the Mystery of Incarnation

Mentors behave with humility before the mystery of Jesus the Christ. They are not dogmatic or judgmental. They do not try to reduce faith to words, creeds, credentials, or memory verses. Their sense of awe before God is one of the first things people notice about them. The reason why Christian mentors rarely miss an opportunity for weekly worship is that they are compelled by a sense of adoration. They eagerly sing the praises of God, even if they do not fully understand the ways of God. They suffer with the problems of inexplicable evil, but they always cling to non-rational grace.

Although mentors can talk about their own experiences of victory over universal anxieties, they never let that go to their heads. In each category, they model genuine humility.

- They are always ready to learn new things. They demonstrate an uncommon openness to go beyond their comfort zones, associate with strange people, immerse themselves in different cultures, and understand different religions. Yes, they can encourage others to overcome emptiness and meaninglessness, but mentors are constantly learning new perspectives and ideas.

- They are always aware of their personal limitations. They know that every personality, including their own, has both strengths and weaknesses. They wrestle with, and accept, their own shortcomings. They frankly admire the good and greatness in others. Yes, they can empower others to overcome fears of fate and death, but frankly admit they are still only human.

- They are always compelled to confess. They own their mistakes and are aware of their essential imperfections. They acknowledge that they are worse human beings than they even realize. They come to God confessing (in the words of the old campfire song) *"it's me, it's me, it's me, O Lord; standing in the need of prayer."*

If you are considering your own call to mentor, then answer for yourself these questions. Are you curious? Are you habitually learning new things, befriending new people, mingling with different cultures, and being respectful of other races? And are you self-aware? Do you recognize your own shortcomings? Are you able to accept criticism? Do you genuinely admire people other than yourself? And are you repentant? Do you readily admit mistakes? Do you worship regularly? Do you admit the need for grace?

6) Compulsion for the Redemptive Purpose of God

Mentors have a deep desire to be part of God's plan for redeeming the world. They think of themselves as participants in salvation's history. They may not think of themselves as *leaders*, or *organizers*, or even *proclaimers* of God's redemptive purpose. They may not see themselves as visionaries, administrators, or preachers. They are often very quiet and shun public recognition. Yet they clearly see themselves as participants, and they *desire* to be a part of the emerging and expanding Realm of God.

This element of "desire" is important, because mentoring takes time, and progress is difficult to measure. "Success" is often hidden, and emerges slowly, and in unexpected ways. Mentoring, therefore, requires considerable patience and persistence. Unless the mentor truly *desires* to do it, and *desires* to be a hidden part of God's redemptive purpose, he or she will not have the stamina to keep going.

The redemptive purpose of God is as complex, multi-dimensional, and mysterious as the incarnation of God in Christ. Indeed, in the most profound Christian perspective they are one and the same. God's purpose is to *dwell* among God's people (Rev. 21:3 NRSV). Here are some of the Biblical perspectives on God's redemptive purpose:

Gospels

1) True Justice – Matthew 25:35-46
2) Multiplication of Disciples ("The Great Commission") – Matthew 28:18-20
3) Ultimate Love ("The Great Commandment") – Matthew 22:37-39
4) Ransom for the Captives – Mark 10:45
5) Divine Healing – Luke 9:1-2
6) Heavenly Banquet – Luke 14:1-24
7) Forgiveness and Reunion – Luke 15:32
8) Vindication of the Humble – Luke 18:14
9) Light Overcoming Darkness – John 9:11
10) Abundant Life – John 10:10

11) Resurrection – John 11:25
12) Unity with Christ – John 14:1-5

Epistles

13) Covenant Community – Acts 2:43-47
14) Peace and Equality – Acts 10:34
15) Righteous Judgment – Acts 17:29-31
16) Final Reconciliation – Romans 5:9-11
17) Return to Eden – Romans 8:19-25
18) Understanding and Love – 1 Corinthians 13:12-13
19) Real Resurrection – 1 Corinthians 15:51-58
20) Sacred Sanctuary – Hebrews 9:5-28
21) Spiritual "House" – 1 Peter 2:1-3
22) Children of God – 1 John 3:1-10
23) Perfect Love – 1 John 4:7-21
24) New Jerusalem – Revelation 21:1-27

Do any of these perspectives on the redemptive purpose of God stir your heart, move you to tears and make you laugh for joy, or fill you with a desire to help? These are the compulsions of a mentor. Mentors do not seek the limelight. They only seek to sit at the feet of the Master ... and to draw more disciples into the Master's company.

7) Recognition that You Are Already a Mentor

The more you reflect on it, the more surprised you become. You began in skepticism. You felt you did not deserve to be a mentor, and listed any number of reasons why you should not be a mentor. Some of your reasons were, in fact, quite probably valid. Some of them were borne out of fear and selfishness. Then you began to really think about it:

✓ Yes, I do have memories of having been mentored at various times in my life.
✓ Yes, I do remember experiences of the Holy when God profoundly impacted my life.
✓ Yes, I do have experience with systems of accountability, and am not afraid of being held accountable.
✓ Yes, weak as I am, I do have personal experiences of victory that I can describe.
✓ Yes, I really do stand in awe of Christ, and do not pretend to know everything.

✓ Yes, I really do desire to participate in God's purpose to redeem the world.

As proof of these facts, you suddenly realize that *you are already treated as a mentor by others.* Family members look to you for advice. Co-workers share confidences with you. Friends and neighbors seek you out amid the struggles and uncertainties of life. Complete strangers speak to you in airports and during soccer games. You may even run from it, but mentoring moments keep finding you. You may decline to talk with people, but they keep coming to you. You may be fearful of the risks of being wrong, but you are compelled to help people do what is right.

The call to mentor is compelling "in spite of everything." You can't seem to escape it or excuse yourself from it. Even though you also have memories of emptiness, fears of death, and problems with guilt, and even though you also have experiences of defeat, and continue to struggle to know God, and even though selfishness continues to lead you astray just like everyone else … *in spite of all that* you still feel the urgency to help others overcome despair, feel the touch of God, and follow their destinies.

You do not choose to be a mentor in the same way that you "choose" a course of study or a career. You simply find yourself doing it. You just have to do it. In this sense, the call to mentoring is a lot like the call to parenting. Most people do not "choose" to be a parent, and even if they think they are in control of the process, they soon learn otherwise. You do not become pregnant and then have second thoughts. Once you have a child, you don't wake up each morning judiciously considering whether you should give the child toilet training, buy the child new clothes, guide the child to get along with other kids, or help the child take responsibility for his or her own life.

Parenting, like mentoring, does not really depend on your sense of competence. No matter how much training you think you have had for childbirth, or how many books and courses you have taken in child psychology, or how much "experience" you have had dealing with other people's kids, the reality is that you will awaken each morning doubting your ability to do it. Sure, there will be times (ages and phases) when you think you are more or less able, but the chronic condition of parenting is your sense that you don't deserve to be a parent. You are essentially incompetent. You live in the fear of making mistakes, but you can't just decide not to try anymore. God has given you this child, and to shirk your responsibility with some feeble claim of being ill-prepared or too immature yourself won't work. You don't really have a choice.

It is this combined sense of intimacy and responsibility that explains why ancient Christian mentors often referred to the people they mentored as sons or daughters. Consider Paul's relationship with Timothy:

> But Timothy's worth you know, how as a son with a father he has served with me in the gospel. (Phil. 2:22)

> This charge I commit to you, Timothy, my son, in accordance with the prophetic utterances which pointed to you, that inspired by them you may wage the good warfare, holding faith and a good conscience. (1 Tim. 1:18-19)

> You then, my son, be strong in the grace that is in Christ Jesus, and what you have heard from me before many witnesses entrust to faithful men who will be able to teach others also. (2 Tim. 2:1-2)

Whoever authored the epistles that we have in the New Testament, it is clear that such letters were part of a larger mentoring process.

> By Silvanus, a faithful brother as I regard him, I have written briefly to you, exhorting and declaring that this is the true grace of God; stand fast in it. She who is at Babylon [Rome], who is likewise chosen, sends you greetings; and so does my son Mark. Greet one another with the kiss of love. Peace to all of you that are in Christ. (1 Pet. 5:12-14)

> You are witnesses, and God also, how holy and righteous and blameless was our behavior to you believers; for you know how, like a father with his children, we exhorted each one of you and encouraged you and charged you to lead a life worthy of God, who calls you into his own kingdom and glory. (1 Thess. 2:10-12)

The relationship of mentoring was experienced much like the relationship of a parent and child, and there was a natural progression by which, through baptism, people were "born again," "adopted as children of God," and henceforth "brothers and sisters" with the true Son and family of God.

The dawning realization that, despite all of your inadequacies, God is already using you as a mentor comes as both confirmation and shock. It's no use running from it. Now is the time to work backwards to prayerfully reconsider the previous seven "indicators" that you really are called to mentor. You will seek out mentors for yourself, or intensify your training with a current mentor. Your mentor can help you learn from your own past, remember experiences of the Holy, participate in systems of accountability, celebrate spiritual victories, humble yourself before the incarnation, and sharpen your desire to be part of God's redemptive purpose. What you learn from your mentor, you pass on to those whom you mentor. That is the essence of apostolic succession. It is the real core of disciple making. It is not from Sunday school, Christian education courses, or seminaries that Christian leaders emerged. It is from the choice of God and the relationship of mentoring.

Snapshot

I think it was my Spanish language teacher who first revealed to me the potential and calling of Christian mentoring. He saw in me a restless, reflective, artistic, physically unimpressive lad of 14 with a history of being bullied, and a suppressed anger toward the world. We were thrown together in one of the most affluent suburbs north of Chicago — a place noted for its elite education, perfect football seasons, and professionally successful graduates. Of course, we never actually talked about religion. We did read and discuss the great literature of Cervantes and Lope de Vega, Mariano Azuela, and the existentialism of Unamuno and Ortega y Gasset. He used the discipline of learning Spanish to force me to choose my words, assemble my thoughts, and explore hidden meaning. He did this with a sense of irony and optimism that motivated me to do more than learn a language.

Another important experience of mentoring has been with Paul Tillich and his disciples. I never actually studied with Tillich, of course, since he died about the time that I was studying Spanish in High School. My Spanish teacher let me go once I graduated, but intellectually "handed me off" to Tillich. His life and teaching became central to my life and doctoral research. I wrote my dissertation with one of his students, and have known and appreciated many more. Tillich helped me explore the existential anxieties that permeate my life, and discern the various ways in which God is incarnate to give hope. He helped me explore my authenticity as a person. Through his own interpersonal failures and ethical triumphs in life, he guided me to confront hidden manipulations and temptations.

Despite these influences, I never thought I could or would be a mentor. I thought, *Who, me? I could never be as compassionate, insightful, or spiritual as the people who have mentored me!* A great awakening occurred in seminary. I was a youth pastor in what was even then a rare, growing, vital congregation outside Philadelphia. We had a large and dynamic youth ministry, the cornerstone of which was music. Our youth performed and sang contemporary Christian music all over the region. Our weekly rehearsals intentionally combined vigorous conversation about scripture, deep prayer for one another, and sensitivity to the Holy Spirit ... along with practice, practice, and more practice.

During one of our road trips, the group sang at a hospital. Unfortunately, no one had told us that it was a chronic care mental hospital, and the experience was shattering to many of the sheltered kids in our group. On the ride home, I spent several hours kneeling on the cold metal floor of the school bus, moving from row to row of weeping kids who were overcome with grief, confusion, and questions about the truth and purpose of life.

Now, I had been trained to teach, coach, and counsel ... but not to mentor. This was a situation that called for mentoring. A brief discourse on the history of the problem of evil was not helpful. A pep talk about God's eventual victory over death, or extra training on how to relate to mentally and emotionally challenged people, was equally useless. Therapeutic counseling to help kids articulate their issues and resolve their emotions might be helpful later, but it couldn't be done in five minutes kneeling on the floor of the bus. And even if it could, it wouldn't really answer their questions, and I doubted that I would ever be a sufficient source of counseling for them anyway.

What was needed was mentoring. From that day, my relationship with individual youth in the group changed. We began a long and intentional conversation about the experience of Christ, spiritual habits for daily living, our authenticity as human beings, the temptations and manipulations that stopped our perpetual growth, the accountability of faith, and the personal destiny that God has in store for each one of us. Eventually, of course, I moved on. They let me go, and I let them go. Twenty years later, I received an email in response to one of my books from a military chaplain deployed in whatever war zone was going on overseas. "Are you the Tom Bandy who was in a youth group at X church near Philadelphia in the 1970's?" I confirmed that I was, indeed, that Tom Bandy, and he responded saying, "I was a member of your youth group. Just wanted to say thanks!"

Got Mentoring?
All Those Who Want Mentoring, Please Raise Your Hands

Mentoring is counter-cultural to the modern world. If you are a mentor (whether you like it or not) then you are probably already feeling maverick to modern educational and church institutions. The adrenaline rush of rebellion passes in a few days, and you are probably left feeling a consistent, low-level discomfort with your working environment. It should be no surprise, therefore, that seekers looking for mentoring will be reluctant to raise their hand in class, sign up on the bulletin board, or write their names on a piece of paper and pass them forward on the offering plate during worship.

On the one hand, you have to seek out the seekers. Develop the habit of having intentional, open-ended conversations. These are non-judgmental and gentle conversations that elicit deeper sharing, and encourage others to speak honestly. It is important that you match vulnerability with vulnerability. In other words, you never invite others to reveal themselves unless you are ready to reveal yourself *to the same degree of stress.* The basic pattern of conversation, which may be improvised and repeated many ways, looks like this:

1) Affirmation
2) Compatibility
3) Question
4) Variation
5) Invitation

This sequence is at the core of a larger acquaintanceship. Usually you have already met and talked about matters of mutual interest. This could involve work, hobbies, lifestyles, and perspectives on anything from child-rearing to politics to art. This acquaintanceship is never feigned. It is genuine. It is the natural first step toward friendship. If there is nothing of common interest to talk about, you may not become friends anyway. There is nothing wrong with that. When people intuit this lack of common interest, they usually part company with respect and nothing more.

There is, however, a "mentoring alternative" in every conversation. At the point where most people are deciding whether there is a potential friendship there or not, people called to mentoring see another possibility. There is another option. It is a variation in the relationship that may, or may not, involve "friendship," but has a unique potential beyond or alongside "friendship." For example:

Alex and Carlos both participate in a service club or church committee. They are different ages, with different professions and incomes, and probably have different family experiences and personal histories. Alex seeks out seekers in every conversation. Once they begin talking over coffee after church, they establish some minimal grounds for common interest, but both are unclear whether there is a friendship forming. Alex deliberately turns the conversation in a new direction.

- ✓ **Affirmation:** Alex expresses his admiration or appreciation for something Carlos has said or done. Perhaps it was a daring idea, or perhaps it was a spontaneous behavior pattern, but Alex lifts it up to affirm Carlos' integrity or expertise. Remember, this is genuine. If there is nothing to affirm, don't make it up. Don't exaggerate it. Just be honest.

- ✓ **Compatibility:** The two of them may discuss Alex's affirmation for a time. Carlos may be surprised or embarrassed, or may seek more information or insight. Now Alex matches the stress level Carlos is feeling. He shares something similar from his own life, and some of the positive or negative consequences he experienced from it. Remember, the stress level or degree of vulnerability matches that of Carlos. Alex does not reveal *less* of himself than Carlos did of himself, which would make Carlos feel nervous. He also does not reveal *more* of himself than Carlos did, which would make Carlos feel evaluated.

- ✓ **Question:** The two of them may talk about Alex's experience for a time, but eventually Alex poses a question inspired by the conversation. It is always an open-ended question, which is to say that there are genuinely different ways to answer it. "What does it mean that …?" "What do you think might happen if …?" "How does this fit with what my father taught, or what my preacher preached, or what some book advocated …?" This is a genuine question for which Alex does not have a pat answer. It takes their relationship to a new level — not so much a level of mutual affection, but rather a level of mutual exploration.

✓ **Variation:** Carlos may respond to Alex in many ways. He may repeat some dogmatism or aphorism. He may offer some hesitant speculation. He may declare his indifference. He may politely excuse himself and walk away. *If he stays*, however, Alex responds with an alternative answer. He does not claim it to be the only answer, and it may be a tentative answer, but it is an honest and personal answer. Alex implies that Carlos is free to respond, or not respond, without harm. Again, Alex's degree of vulnerability has matched Carlos' degree of vulnerability, but has also conveyed his readiness to go deeper.

✓ **Invitation:** Alex invites Carlos into a mentoring conversation. "Would you like to go deeper …?" "Would you like to know more …?" "Would you like to explore where you are going, what is holding you back, what the consequences might be …?" The invitation may be too much for a *single* conversation, and perhaps it will only occur once Alex and Carlos have had several more conversations over coffee, with each one probing deeper. It is astonishing, however, how often this does happen in a single conversation. This reveals both the urgency of seekers today who are looking for mentors, and how the personality or integrity of the mentor is revealed quickly and intuitively in unspoken ways.

This conversation does not occur in a vacuum. There is a larger context of credibility that Alex has shaped, or that the Holy Spirit has shaped around Alex. It would not be surprising, for example, if later we learned that Carlos had been aware of Alex prior to this conversation. Carlos had observed him, overheard him, or heard about him. Or it would not be surprising that during ongoing conversations that improvised on the affirmation-compatibility and question-variation themes, Carlos had quietly asked questions from trusted friends or colleagues about Alex's integrity, trustworthiness, and motivations.

So, while on the one hand you must seek out seekers through intentional conversations, on the other hand you have to allow seekers to seek you out. This requires more than patience. It requires a discipline of modeling a spiritual life. The combination of predictable behavior in daily living, and daring action in exceptional or stressful circumstances, earns Alex a reputation. He unconsciously behaves respectfully and gently with colleagues, neighbors, and complete strangers. He is always the one to step to the side and make room for a newcomer in the circle of conversation. He is always the one to control his temper and intercede for reconciliation. He is also the one who takes a stand for ethical practice in the midst of opportunism. He is also the one with whom people share confidences and test new ideas. Alex has a reputation for having spiritual habits, judicious insights, and careful relationships.

Credibility attracts conversation. The hunger for mentoring leads people to make assumptions about credibility based on the smallest clues. Complete strangers will share remarkably personal things at an airport, bus terminal, or transportation center, or at sports arena, pub, or coffee shop, or anywhere anonymous where people simultaneously lose their inhibitions and feel lost in their identity. Their only clues may be the mannerisms, dress, or overhead comments from people who give the appearance of integrity. Such a thin layer of confidence rarely leads to profound mentoring, but how others observe your spontaneous behavior and daring deeds often opens the door to the conversational cycle of affirmation, compatibility, question, variation, and invitation.

Transition points and boundary situations are the contexts in which most mentoring relationships are born. Figuratively speaking, these are often the "bus stations" where people are transferring from one stage of life to another, or the "borders" between one state and another, when people are apt to reveal their "passports" of identity. Transition points and boundary situations precipitate questions about integrity, loyalty, self-confidence, and purpose.

It is increasingly common for churches to assign adult "mentors" for teenagers during the confirmation or catechism process. The process often feels institutional and artificial, but even then it is remarkably effective in deepening the Christian maturity of young adults. Note that churches often discover that the available pool of adult "mentors" is remarkably small, since most of the adults need mentoring themselves. The mentors are often grandparents who successfully overcame post-war anxieties to lead healthy and successful lives, and the mentored are often teens from healthy families who are inclined to venerate the wisdom of older, optimistic survivors. The transitional moment is the shift from adolescence to adulthood, and the church uses the rite of confirmation as a vehicle for a mentoring moment. It may or may not be particularly successful — partly because the goal is unclear — but we catch a glimpse of the context for mentoring opportunities.

There are certain kinds of people who are most earnest in their search for mentoring. They are often under 45. They may be late "baby boomers" that missed the wave of opportunity and are struggling to catch up. They may be "baby busters" who are struggling with the social context of frustration and cynicism left behind by the boomer generation. Or they may be "echoes" that are unsure who to imitate, and are even less clear about being themselves. Previous generations tended to prefer the extremes of either private religion or large groups. Successive generations have preferred small groups, then cell groups, then peer groups, then friendship circles, and intimate one-to-one relationships that help in their search for personal reinforcement and individual guidance.

The emerging leaders of tomorrow are not coming out of standardized education curriculums, large mega-churches, or even professional programs. All of these are relevant to leadership training, but in themselves have been remarkably unsuccessful in birthing leaders. There are patterns to discern in the people who are looking for mentoring. They are all people who are taking time out, or prioritizing time to be apart, from traditional educational, ecclesiastical, or business institutions. The following describe the signs of interest.

First, their interest in scripture, biography, or spirituality has suddenly accelerated. They seem to be paying more attention to sermons, attending study groups, or reading scripture on their own. They are fascinated by the life stories of ancient or contemporary spiritual leaders. They are reading more widely about world religions and spiritual practices.

This acceleration of interest in sacred writings, sacred people, or sacred journeys often seems dramatic, because they may be starting at ground zero. Since the decline of the liberal arts in the late 1960's, many professionals do not have the faintest sense of history, have minimal abilities to appreciate art, and have little acquaintance with literature. While fantastic and outlandish religious speculation has sharpened their distrust of religious institutions, it has also awakened their hearts to believe in a meaning beyond materialism.

Second, their emotional engagement with mission has suddenly increased. They not only seem better informed about global and local events, but they also weep, anger, and argue with greater passion. They seem to be searching for the right social service opportunity, more frustrated with administrative meetings, and ready to experiment with new ideas.

The renewed engagement with mission resembles the excitement around the Peace Corps, or the passion around the civil rights movements of the 60's and early 70's, but it is at once more ambitious and more personal.

It is ambitious in that it inter-connects ethical, environmental, political and spiritual systems. *Start making a difference here, and eventually you will make a difference in everything, everywhere.* Therefore, mission is more personal. It is more important to *do* something hands-on than merely raise money or make board policy.

Third, they have begun to question their career paths. They may not actually be planning on changing jobs, but they are restless with the same routine. They are less interested in process and more interested in end results. Making money has got to have a more personal payoff. They want their work-lives to be more fulfilling.

This integration of work and play is part of a holistic approach to living. There is no longer a clear division between work time, family time, and recreation time. Flexible work schedules, advance communication technologies, and the overall speed of change and opportunity have forced people to live *one* life rather than separate lives. Therefore, career *and* meaning must happen in the same time frame. Wealth, security, independence ... *and* justice, hope, and peace ... must be reunited in the weekly calendar.

Fourth, they have intentionally or unintentionally added stress to their intimate relationships. They have distanced themselves from old friends, and become acquainted with people beyond their normal circles. They are entering a new stage of parenting. Their spouses are beginning to worry that they are no longer quite the same people.

All of these changes have placed people at a turning point in their lives, which may threaten (or promise) changes in the lives of their intimates. Intimacy may be broken or enhanced, but the outcome is unclear. Friendship, marriage, and even family responsibility toward parents and children are no longer ends in themselves, but only a means toward deeper meaning, clearer purpose, and a larger, global harmony.

Fifth, they have inadvertently become part of a *third culture* in the turmoil of immigration and emigration. I borrow the term from Dave Gibbons, who says: "Third culture is the mindset and will to love, learn, and serve in any culture, even in the midst of pain and discomfort."[5] People's identities are neither defined by first generation loyalties to the origins of parents and grandparents, nor by second generation adaptation to the

---

[5] Dave Gibbons, *The Monkey and the Fish: Liquid Leadership for a Third-Culture Church* (Grand Rapids: Zondervan, 2009), 38.

customs of a new country. They are defined by the scramble to maintain identity in multiple cultures simultaneously.

All of these changes suggest that people who seek mentoring are no longer driven by a desire *to belong*. They are driven by the reality of being *on the boundary*. They have consciously or unconsciously concluded that the best they can do is *partially belong*, and that they will in fact "belong" to multiple groups, relationships, occupations, habits, and obligations. They no longer insist or expect that their lives will be consistent. Contradiction and ambiguity are inevitable. If they cannot reconcile everything, at least they can cope with integrity and align themselves with a greater destiny.

It can be argued that the foregoing description defines post-modern living in general. However, not all people seek mentoring. Many continue to live in the convictions of modernity, and therefore continue to believe that educational programs, career paths, and occasional psychotherapy will lead to a happy and well-adjusted life. Many others have begun to doubt all of this, but are not very far along in understanding the implications. They may not yet be at a transition in life or at a boundary of experience, and wealth, health, and relationships may allow them to maintain a "dreaming innocence."[6]

The signs of interest in mentoring represent a kind of hierarchy of awareness. The more that unconscious intuitions become conscious insights, the more restless post-modern people become, and the more urgent they become in their search for mentors.

- Awareness begins with accelerated interest in sacred writings, spiritual personalities, religious perspectives, and the history of ideas. This may initially be satisfied by a community college course, a book club, or a church study program, but the restlessness persists as people wonder at the existential "stake" revealed in the pursuit of truth, beauty, and virtue.

- Awareness deepens through engagement with hands-on social service, such as a local, regional or global mission. This may initially be satisfied with a social service project, a charitable vacation, or by the investment of spare time to care for the "under

---

[6] "Dreaming Innocence" is a term borrowed from my mentor Paul Tillich, which he used in a similar way to describe the boundary situation of existence. See *Systematic Theology*, Vol. 2 (Chicago: University Press, 1957), 33-36.

privileged," but the restlessness persists as people experience gratuitous evil and radical generosity, and ask questions they have never asked before.

- Awareness deepens yet again as people question their own career paths, corporate loyalties, and life priorities. This may initially be satisfied by a change of occupation or early retirement, but the restlessness persists as people discover that these changes precipitate more anxieties than they resolve. Ambiguity is inescapable in the best corporations and altruistic retirement plans.

It is often at this point that the desire for mentoring becomes clear in the consciousness of post-modern people. They are no longer looking for teachers, mission coordinators, or corporate gurus and self-help books. They realize the need to associate themselves with someone who can cope with the ambiguities and align themselves with a higher purpose.

- Now awareness becomes urgent as people add stress to their intimate relationships. This may initially be satisfied by psychotherapy and marital counseling, or by reshaping circles of intimacy or divorce, but the restlessness persists precisely because true love would rather adapt than give up. The mentoring relationship expands awareness of how to love, and of how to participate in the spiritual journey of the beloved.

Notice that the heightened awareness of the need for mentoring does not reach its peak of urgency even with the stress of intimate relationships. The last tie to modernity is cut when even sexual or parental intimacy is no longer ultimate. Even the "family" becomes a means to an end, rather than an end in itself.

- Awareness peaks with the realization that the emerging generations are a "third culture" that exists "in between" or "on the boundary of" many distinct and equally valuable cultures. Individuals either establish an identity and purpose with reference to absolutes beyond the diversity of cultures, or they lose themselves to the clash of cultures.

This final awareness fuels the earnestness of mentoring. Mentoring that started from a simple conversation, and which may have been pursued sporadically over time, becomes ever more serious and urgent.

Here we come back to the question of how one even finds people to mentor. Seekers of mentoring don't tend to raise their hand sign up on a list, register for a course, or phone to make an appointment. They are out there, in increasing numbers, with varying degrees of awareness and urgency. People who seek mentoring are in a similar quandary to people who offer mentoring. Seekers soon discover that Sunday worship rarely leaders to mentoring (although it might lead to education). There is no institution where you can sign up, there is no course that you can take, and there is no professional with whom you can make an appointment. Mentoring just doesn't work that way. Unlike the ancient world, the modern world does not intentionally provide opportunities for masters and disciples to get together. Indeed, the modern world lives in denial that mentoring is a genuine need.

That is why seekers and mentors go searching on the edges of education or on the peripheries of institutions. They hang about the church, but don't join, because their goal is to connect with a mentor rather than to serve a committee. They take a course from the community college so that they can legitimately lurk in the common room and cafeteria where they might fall into interesting conversations. Since mentoring is most likely to feel urgent in times of transition or boundary testing, seekers and mentors tend to circle around places of transition and boundary testing, such as:

- Transportation and communication hubs
- Sports arenas, fitness centers, and meditation centers
- Coffee shops, wine bars, and restaurants
- Theaters, art exhibits, and cinemas

Wherever people gather to expand relationships, try on new attitudes, explore different perspectives, connect with different cultures, and generally expand their horizons, there you will probably find seekers and mentors looking for one another. When you think about it, much of our time is spent enjoying or protecting our comfort zones. Mentoring connections, however, lie just outside of our comfort zones. With one foot in safe territory, the other foot probing unexplored country, seekers and mentors live a tentative, intuitive, risky kind of lifestyle. It may take a lot of courage for a seeker, and a lot of patience for a mentor.

How do you market mentoring? How do you advertise, especially in an environment of skepticism? The dilemma seems similar to the challenge faced by milk producers in recent years. Given all the better tasting choices of beverages, how could the milk industry lure consumers to buy their product? Of course milk was *healthier* than almost any other beverage, but even orange juice had a prettier color.

Got Milk? The marketing campaign they used was humorous, quirky, young, hip, and rhythmic. It managed to connect traditional values with contemporary relevance, old folk wisdom with young folk vitality, and cows, corn, and tractors with cultures, good company, and fast cars. Suddenly the barn was a transportation hub and the meeting place of people looking for a good thing. I often think that mentors ... and churches that want to promote mentoring ... could learn from the marketing of milk.

The fact that mentors (even reluctant mentors) feel compelled to go out and look for people to mentor indicates that they are not quite ready to mentor in the first place. Their attitude still betrays the lingering assumption of modernity that mentoring, like education, is a matter of professionalism and programming. We assume that the best way to mentor is through a classroom that students must "attend," through a curriculum that students must "obtain," or through a degree program that students must "earn." The modern world understands "vocation" differently than the pre- or post-modern world. The vocation of mentoring for modernity was an orderly career path, whereas the vocation of mentoring for post-modernity is a deliberate lifestyle. One may earn a living as an educator, but one does not earn a living as a mentor. Indeed, if one did earn a living as a mentor, one would no longer be an effective mentor.

The challenge of mentoring is not to find people to mentor, but to place oneself at the mercy of the Spirit. The Holy Spirit shapes your life, but also shapes the circumstances in which you live. There is no such thing as "coincidence" for those called as mentors. There is only "providence." Even the most casual acquaintance is pregnant with spiritual possibilities. You do not find seekers. Seekers find you. Or, more accurately, the Holy Spirit creates situations in which seekers and mentors find each other. It just happens. The more one surrenders to the Spirit, and shapes the spiritual life, the more mentoring conversations just seem to occur. Sometimes they span a few minutes and sometimes they span a lifetime. Always they are beyond our complete control.

Mentors must get past the compulsion to "go out and look for seekers," just as they must differentiate between mentoring and educating. The "teacher/student" dichotomy must be replaced by a "mentor/seeker" cycle. Mentors become seekers, and seekers become mentors. The best mentors often describe themselves as the most avid seekers. The ones who know the most are often the ones that confess they know the least, and yet the very least that they know is still more than the seeker seeks. The most effective mentors are also being mentored. They are being mentored by others wiser than themselves, or by others more innocent than themselves. This is precisely the situation of most seekers. All alike are being mentored by the Spirit of God.

Snapshot

I travel a lot. Over the years I have had many unexpected mentoring opportunities. Some lasted for only the duration of an air flight. I remember the nervous young woman in the window seat next to me as we took off from a particularly windy tarmac in Dallas. Her lips smiled as she asked, "Do you think if this plane crashes I might come back as a cat?" Her eyes, however, were quite serious. Why did she ask me this question? Perhaps I was just an unthreatening, old, balding guy in a suit who resembled her father. Perhaps she was responding to my now unconscious spiritual habit to hold a crucifix in my hand, close my eyes, and pray for strangers, whenever a seat belt sign comes on. Whatever the motivation, we talked about God and her coming job interview for the duration of the flight.

Most opportunities for mentoring do not come intentionally. This is contrary to what I was always taught, and how I always thought. I was taught to be "intentional." That is, I was taught to prepare myself ahead of time, actively look for an opportunity to intervene, and then say the magic words, or repeat the memorized scripture, or offer some dramatic gesture that would precipitate intense dialogue and result in dramatic conversion. That might have worked in the Christendom world in which I grew up. It does not work in the pagan world in which I live now. That method is too aggressive, intrusive, and alarming for others. And to be honest, it is too confrontational and scary for an extreme introvert like me. It would leave others feeling annoyed and me feeling guilty.

Mentoring opportunities are not intentional. They are intuitional. You do not seek them out. They seek you out. You do not create them. They capture you. Mentoring opportunities emerge as you pursue the spiritual life. The more that you intuit the real presence of Christ through disciplined spiritual practices, become self-aware of your own strengths and weaknesses, personally wrestle with manipulation and temptation, and focus entirely on God's purpose for your own life, the more you will find yourself in mentoring situations.

I once had the privilege to study with the great New Testament scholar Mathew Black in St. Mary's College, Scotland. A large group had assembled in the Common Room, including many visiting arts students. I don't remember why we were together, but in those days divinity students all wore black gowns with embroidered St. Andrew Crosses, and arts students all wore scarlet gowns with velvet fringe, so it was clear which students belonged to which group. On one side of the room, some ecclesiastical VIP was surrounded by a small group dressed in black. He wore an immaculately white clergy collar and an enormous silver cross, combed his silver hair to look like Lord Byron, and spoke loudly and often in a stentorian voice. On the other side of the room, Professor Black sat surrounded by scarlet gowns. Aside from his stained and badly frayed black gown, there was nothing remarkable about his appearance at all except his posture. He was always leaning forward, listening, and spoke with a remarkable economy of precisely chosen words. The difference between "sanctimonious" and "spiritual" may seem subtle to Christians, but it is as obvious as night and day to seekers.

Sanctimonious people operate from a script and seem pushy. Spiritual people act on intuition, as if guided by an unseen hand, and seem receptive. There is a reason that saints are often painted in ordinary clothes, but with a halo of light surrounding their persons. That is their spirituality. They are not focused on themselves, nor are they even concerned about how others perceive them. They are focused entirely on being connected with the real presence of Jesus Christ. They lose themselves, and they often lose a sense of their own surroundings. They are most *intentional* about their relationship with God. Seekers are attracted to the aura of spirituality just as moths are attracted to light.

Intentionality about God makes mentors intuitional about people. Seekers take the initiative, but once a seeker opens a conversation or attracts attention, mentors intuit the motivation of a seeker and sometimes even the questions in their heart. The seeker may say they want to talk about this and that, but the mentor very quickly discerns that what they *really* want to talk about is something quite different. Mentoring opportunities most often come when you are not looking for them, but looking to God. So don't worry about what you are to say, *for the Holy Spirit will teach you at that very hour what you ought to say* (Luke 12:12).

Walk With Me

A beloved son comes to his father, troubled and anxious over the ambiguities, sorrows, or challenges of living. Perhaps the son has returned from university, survived a broken relationship, resigned from a difficult job, received an unexpected health report, or is simply depressed by the news reports he encounters. The father welcomes him, but feels the strain of his own limited knowledge. He does not have all the answers. He only has the experience of survival, the maturity of hope, and a limitless compassion for his son. This is not a time for lectures. A single room, or a single environment, provides insufficient room for the Holy Spirit to work between them. The father puts on his coat and hat, saying *Come! Walk with me!* It is in the walking, amid the changing scenes that stroke all five senses, that the sixth sense of intuition or insight is sharpest.

Jesus did much the same thing. When he bid Peter or James or John to follow, he was saying the same thing: *Walk with me!* Even when Jesus appeared to Paul on the Damascus Road, the first commandment he gave was for Paul to seek out the mentoring of Ananias, and from there to go into the desert to be alone with Jesus. *Walk with me!* The Gospels are really a synopsis of several journeys around the block. Only the highlights are given. Many more words were said as Jesus traveled with them. Many things diverted Jesus' attention from the conversation (the healing of one person, the confrontation of some injustice, etc.), but it is clear that these were not really diversions at all. Rather, they were ways for the Holy Spirit to enhance the mentoring conversation that took place sitting under trees, sailing on boats, and walking down dusty roads.

The "father/son" conversation may just as well be a "mother/daughter" conversation, but I choose the "parent/child" metaphor because it illustrates the unbalanced relationship between mentor and seeker. There is always a bond of compassion, and there are always opportunities for the parent to learn as well as the child, but the relationship between mentor and seeker is always unequal by virtue of experience. The mentor has always walked more miles, experienced more good and more evil, faced more challenges, and broken through to more victories than the seeker. This does not mean the mentor is perfect, just as the father or mother is not perfect, but it does mean that the mentor's insight and counsel has more weight. Mentor and seeker are humble before the Spirit, but the seeker is additionally humble in listening to the mentor. There is dialogue, but it is not arrogant dialogue, and it is not the dialogue of equals.

Modernity encourages egalitarian thinking. Pre- and post-modernity do not. This is not to say that some individuals are superior because of family connections, income, education, race or any demographic distinctiveness. It recognizes degrees of maturity. It recognizes that some people seem closer to the real presence of God than others ... through self-discipline, suffering the vicissitudes of life, philosophical insight, revelatory experience, or for some other reason. Seekers are looking for mentors ... not just another seeker. What advantage is there in spending time with another seeker, who shares our struggles and shares our questions, other than mutual support and commiseration? No amount of dialogue between two such seekers will lift them from despair or give them new direction. It is like alcoholics commiserating with each other at the local bar. Neither can ultimately help the other. Individually or together they must seek out someone who is sober.

The template of alcohol addiction and intervention is another helpful way to understand the relationship between seeker and mentor. The seeker is an alcoholic ... but the mentor is a *recovering* alcoholic. It is the experience of *recovery* that sets them apart. In the arrogance of alcoholism, the alcoholic often exclaims: *You're no better than me!* In a sense he is right, but in a more profound sense he is wrong. The *recovering* alcoholic is *always better* than the alcoholic. Until the alcoholic recognizes this fact, there can be no mentoring relationship. The mentoring relationship is always unequal.

This point needs to be underlined, because modern people typically balk at this relational inequity. They insist that dialogue cannot be authentic unless the partners are "equal." This gives the would-be seeker an excuse to avoid taking responsibility for learning, and it gives the would-be mentor an excuse to avoid taking responsibility for teaching. If the recovering mentor is really no different than the alcoholic seeker, then the seeker has no real incentive to stop drinking. If the alcoholic seeker is really no different than the recovering mentor, then the mentor has no real responsibility for the health or sobriety of another human being. The mentoring relationship will go nowhere, although a recovering alcoholic who refuses to take responsibility to help another addict may well decide drinking is OK anyway.

In mentoring relationships, authentic dialogue is always "unequal." The seeker cannot do anything else than speak from a context of greater separation from God; the mentor cannot do anything else than speak from a context of greater experience of God. To do otherwise is pretense, and an attempt to escape responsibility for our actions or responsibility for the well-being of others.

Mentoring conversations are unique among the many ways people talk together. These conversations are not about trading opinions, and they are not intended to end in a friendly handshake as we agree to disagree. Mentoring conversations are about sharing insights about truths that are larger than anyone's point of view, and more enduring than anyone's lifespan. The insights of the mentor are certainly not absolute, but they point to something else that is. The seekers participate because they sense, even if they do not quite believe, that there is something greater that lies beyond our subjectivity. They expect a mentor to help them *see more clearly, love more dearly, and follow more nearly, day by day* (to paraphrase a song from the rock opera *Godspell*).[7]

The invitation of the mentor — *Walk with me!* — is expressed in very practical ways. Seeker and mentor promise to participate in a companionship that may be informally or formally expressed in a covenant. For example, they may agree to a timeline of conversation of three to six months, always with an option to extend their "travels." During that time they will:

- meet weekly, at a convenient time and location, for face-to-face conversation;
- exchange emails frequently to share questions, reflections, and insights;
- text message daily with words of encouragement;
- parallel spiritual practices by reading the same sources, or following the same prayer cycle;
- sit together in Sunday worship and de-brief together afterward; and
- intentionally evaluate the mentoring relationship to improve communication or avoid sidetracks.

The mentoring journey is loosely structured, sensitive to the mobility of people, but also open to unexpected events and opportunities. Most mentoring is one-to-one because it is constantly nuanced to individual issues and lifestyles, but some mentoring might occur with a small group.

---

[7] *Godspell* lyrics by Stephen Schwartz, 1971.

Given the time investment implied by such a companionship, it is difficult to mentor more than four to six people at any given time.

Mentoring relationships are never tidy or easily controlled. They may start, stop, and start up again — sometimes after considerable time. Mentoring relationships will vary in intensity. There are periods of great emotion, and other periods of calm, and these are not always predictable. Mentoring relationships also vary in the pace of discernment. Sometimes that are periods of great insights and breakthrough moments, and sometimes there are dry periods when it feels like nothing is happening. The seeker may doubt, but the mentor is convinced that the Spirit pervades the entire conversational journey and encourages persistence and patience.

Once the invitation to *walk with me* is given, and some loose structure for the walk is negotiated, the mentor helps the seeker begin the walk with an attitude of expectancy. This is not like strategic planning, when organizers define anticipated measurable results. The "outcomes" of maturity and purpose are not that definite. The journey begins with both mentor and seeker opening themselves to unpredictable change and uncontrollable experiences of the Holy. Well, perhaps they can be *partially* predicted by establishing specific goals, and perhaps they can be *barely* controlled as we manage changes and interpret mysteries. But in the end, nothing is certain except that both mentor and seeker will be different. Whenever we immerse ourselves in the Spirit, everything changes. Education can be controlled, with each stage marked by a graduation ceremony. Mentoring cannot be fully controlled, and there will be advances, reverses, sidetracks, and the occasional retracing of our own steps.

In the next chapter, I will describe the seven stages ("crises," "breakthroughs," or "spurts") that mark the mentoring journey. Such words are just metaphors to describe the flow of personal or spiritual growth in a fundamentally unpredictable process of change. During the walk, however, mentors exercise a certain style or pattern of behavior. John P. Schuster uses language I find particularly helpful. He says that mentors act as "evocateurs" and "provocateurs," and never as "saboteurs" for the journey of growth.[8]

---

[8] John P. Schuster, *Answering Your Call* (San Francisco: Berrett-Koehler Press 2003), 55-107.

Leading Questions

Mentoring conversations are filled with *leading questions*. A leading *question* is open ended, which is to say that it is open to more than one reply. At the same time it is a *leading* question in that it deliberately launches a particular direction of thought. Lawyers are not allowed to "lead the witness," but mentors must "lead the conversation."

What do you think about this? How do you feel about that? Why do you choose one thing rather than another? Who will you influence, and who will influence you? How will you go about it? When will you start, finish, pause, re-evaluate, give up, or change plans? Where will this course of action end up? All these questions shape the mentoring conversation and guide it in specific directions.

Of course the mentor wishes to ask the *right* questions. These would be questions that are revealing and fruitful, and that open new avenues of inquiry. Unfortunately, it is not always easy to know what questions to ask. Questions elicit unexpected responses. They tease out hidden truths, recover lost memories, explore repressed emotions, awaken new ideas, and birth creative plans. Questions force seekers to think for themselves and take responsibility for their own conclusions.

The Socratic Method is most commonly associated with probing questions that are continuously raised until the seeker arrives at insight. Each question elicits a response, which shapes the next question, until something is fully understood. Aristotle used this principle to guide understanding from the general to the particular. The underlying assumption in both Socratic Method and in Jesus' own teaching is that the truth is already *inside you*, hidden in shadow, imperfectly formed, perhaps only a mustard seed that will eventually bear much fruit.

Deep inside, you already know what is good, beautiful, and true, and by asking questions, and wrestling for answers, you will "know" in the pre-modern sense of that word. You will not only comprehend intellectually, but you will align existentially with both a truth and the Truth. "Who do people say that I am?" Jesus asks. "Who do you say that I am?" he asks further. And when the seeker replies, like Peter, saying "You are the Christ," he articulates both a fact and a commitment. Jesus responds, "Blessed are you … for flesh and blood have not revealed this to you. The Father has revealed it to you" (Mat. 16:13-17). Questions assume that in the end you do not know the truth, but the truth knows you.

Challenging Assertions

Mentoring conversations are punctuated by challenging assertions. These may be observations that are deliberately provocative or uncomfortable, but they emerge from carefully listening to the questions and responses that are ongoing in the mentoring relationship. Observations are always offered with reference to the larger context of the seeker's life and environment. They challenge hidden assumptions or biases, illuminate matters of significance for spiritual growth, interpret events with historical or theological principles, and invite discussion or debate.

By asking questions, you imply that the truth is within you. By making assertions, you imply that the truth is out there. Consider this ... consider that. Look at it this way ... look at it that way. Understand these perspectives. Experiment with these choices. Uncover the hidden meaning. Interpret the obvious. Discover the roots, and discern the purpose. Discussions may often be animated, and sometimes pedantic, but all to the point of maturity.

There really is no place for playing "devil's advocate" in a mentoring relationship. There must be no pretense or subterfuge, lest it undermine trust or leave a seeker guessing about the true intentions of the mentor. If role play is helpful to understanding alternative perspectives, it is clearly identified as just that. The conversation must be entirely honest and perhaps uncomfortably honest.

Jesus often spoke in parables and metaphors to challenge the disciples to discern truths for themselves. The parable of the sower (Mark 4) is presented to all, and interpreted to the disciples. Jesus says "He who has ears to hear, let him hear" (Mark 4:9). Even when he speaks to them "plainly," his challenging assertions always encourage further and deeper insight ... and challenge the disciples to take responsibility for their faith. After speaking of the significance of his death, the disciples exclaim "Now you are speaking plainly!" But Jesus challenges their faith, anticipating that their future actions will belie their claims to understand (John 16:22-33).

The goal of the mentoring conversation is not to reach intellectual agreement, but to help seekers think for themselves and take responsibility for their own convictions. Certainly the mentor's ideas and faith will be influential, but mentoring is not about conversion or persuading others to assent to dogmas. We are exploring a larger mystery of truth, which in Christian mentoring is a larger mystery of Christ. The maturity that is sought involves understanding of facts, awareness of self, discernment of truth, and the courage of one's own conviction.

Decisive Interventions

Mentoring relationships are delicate things. There are many ways in which they might break apart in dislike or enmity, or break down into merely friendly conversations or predictable routines. The task of the mentor is to quickly discern the threat, and to take decisive action to confront it. Whenever the relationship seems to have become angry, hostile, or merely emotional, or shallow, unproductive, and boring, there is always some hidden issue that needs to be addressed. There are three kinds of issues that threaten mentoring conversations, and that ultimately sabotage spiritual growth.

- **Deadweights**

   The term "deadweight" was originally a nautical term used to describe the tonnage of a ship (including ballast, crew, and stores) that was *unavailable* for productive use in transporting goods. More recently, the term has been used to describe the stage of a rocket when all the propellant is used up. Ballast is what holds you back; deadweight is what drags you down. You must either lighten the ship or jettison the deadweight of the rocket, or the journey will come to a tragic end.

   The "deadweight" that every person carries will eventually be revealed in the mentoring relationship. Perhaps it is a relationship, personal habit, personality trait, unfulfilling career, unproductive use of time, useless sentiment, unresolved anger, or some other issue in personal, family, business, or recreational life that holds us back from growth. Or perhaps it is a strategy, technique, or behavior pattern that once worked well to further your relationships, career, or stability, but which is no longer effective and is dragging you down.

   In the mentoring relationship with the "rich young ruler," Jesus challenges him to let go of the "deadweight" of wealth, and to follow him, commenting that it is easier for a camel to go through the eye of the needle than for a rich man to enter the Kingdom of God (Mat. 19:16-26). Later Christian experience, particularly in the early monastic tradition, reveals that it may be difficult but not impossible. Ancient Christian mentoring often emphasized the need to free oneself from the "deadweights" of the world (prestige, wealth, power, and so on).

Mentors take decisive action. They identify the deadweight, challenge the seeker, and help the seeker do whatever is necessary to break free. Only then will the journey continue, or will a stable orbit be achieved.

- **Roadblocks**

A roadblock is a barrier that prohibits further progress. The barrier may be natural, like a landslide or a washed out bridge, or the barrier may be strategically placed, like a police blockade or a convoy checkpoint. In any case, one either crosses the barrier or turns back.

Roadblocks inevitably emerge in every mentoring relationship. Perhaps it is a personal tragedy, family crisis, loss of income, religious dogma, deep-seated fear, or unexpected situation that stops spiritual growth. Perhaps it is the ultimatum of a spouse, child, parent, or friend, or the threat of a religious institution, government agenda, or corporation that warns you to turn away from spiritual growth.

Jesus' long-term mentoring relationship with Peter faced constant roadblocks. Even after Jesus' resurrection and "Great Commission," Peter still returned to the obligations of family and the lure of his old occupation. Jesus appears on the seashore to challenge Peter three times: "Simon, do you love me more than these." He then warns him of the threat of martyrdom for the cause (John 1:1-18).

Mentors take decisive action. They analyze the barrier, look for alternative ways around it, and help the seeker take courage to continue the journey and pay the price of spiritual growth.

- **Sidetracks**

A sidetrack is a diversion from the main road that ultimately takes you in the wrong direction. Sometimes travelers miss a turn, sometimes they choose the wrong turn, and sometimes they think they chose the right turn and later discover it was not.

It is not always easy to discern whether a fork in the road is a shortcut or a sidetrack, but mentors must be quick to discern the truth. Perhaps the diversion is another stream of thought, or a different kind of question, or a particular enthusiasm, or an unexpected passion. Perhaps the diversion is another media or method of dialogue. Perhaps the diversion is an excuse to avoid talking about what really matters.

Jesus reserved some of his most uncomfortable remarks to address sidetracks to faithfulness. Even seemingly worthwhile tasks can become sidetracks for spiritual growth. "Let the dead bury their own dead," Jesus says. "No one who puts their hand to the plow and looks back is fit for the Kingdom of God" (Luke 9:59-62).

Mentors must be quick to identify sidetracks that are taking the conversation ... and the seeker ... in the wrong direction. They must explain the mistake, retrace steps to the main road, and reestablish the goals of the mentoring relationship.

All of these deadweights, roadblocks, and sidetracks emerge in every mentoring relationship because inevitably mentoring leads to the stress of change. Schuster's reference to "sabotage" is particularly revealing, because very little of this is mere coincidence. The source of the sabotage is often the seeker personally, and unconscious psychological attitudes or addictive behavior patterns try to halt spiritual growth. The source of sabotage may also be outside forces from marital and family situations, or from corporate and career pressure, or even from religious institutions. Occasionally, the source of sabotage may be the mentor personally, for we are all imperfect.

Interventions may be rare in the mentoring relationship, but they will inevitably be required. No matter how evocative the questions might be, or how provocative the assertions might be, there will be moments when the mentoring relationship itself is in peril by internal or external forces. Mentors act to free the seeker, encourage the seeker, and focus the seeker. They will confront any obstacles that keep the seeker from spiritual growth, even if the obstacles are occasionally the mentors themselves.

Pregnant Silences

Mentoring relationships allow spaces for meditation and reflection. The absence of conversation can sometimes be more fruitful than conversation. Too many words get in the way. Too much time together clouds discernment. The relationship itself gets in the way of personal growth. These spaces of silence may last a few moments or a few weeks or months, and in some mentoring relationships the spaces may last years before the relationship is renewed. However, when the relationship is renewed and conversation begins again, both mentor and seeker realize that something new and deeper has emerged. The conversation does not just carry on from where it ended, but it seems to have taken a leap forward in maturity and understanding.

I often use the terms "mentor" and "midwife" interchangeably. The latter term is a provocative metaphor. Mentors act like midwives in that they use their talents to help people give birth to the mission child that is within every person. Giving birth to maturity may seem a curious paradox, but the experience of realizing unique identity and aligning with God's purpose is akin to birth pangs.

Scholars have difficulty translating the mentoring of Jesus and Nicodemus into English. Jesus speaks of becoming a new creation, and not just about learning new things or adopting new lifestyles. The translations "born again," "born anew," and "born from above" are all accurate, but each captures a different nuance of Jesus' mentoring role (John 3:1-8). What is clear is that the process of being born a second time, like the process of being born the first time, is a combination of joy and pain. Mentors, like midwives, learn when to be gentle, when to be aggressive, and when to do nothing but let nature (and the Spirit) take its course.

Interestingly, Nicodemus appears by name twice more, suggesting a long term conversation with Jesus that has been punctuated by pregnant silences between them. Nicodemus challenges the Pharisees who wish to set aside legal precedents to kill Jesus (John 7:50), and later spares no expense to help Joseph of Arimathea prepare Jesus' body for burial. Ancient tradition suggests that Nicodemus was a highly respected member of the Sanhedrin, became a Christian, and was martyred in the first century. He is venerated as a saint by both the Roman Catholic and Greek Orthodox churches.

In the mentoring relationship, what is unsaid can be just as important as what is said. The gaps can be as profound as the companionship. Mentors are often tempted to "micro-manage" the spiritual growth of seekers, but need to allow space in their relationship. That space, however, is not a matter of indifference. What fills that space are the prayers of the mentor for the seeker, the prayers of the seeker for illumination, and the activity of the Spirit that blows where it chooses —

while mentor and seeker may hear the sound of it, neither knows where it comes or goes (John 3:8).

The "walk" that is shared by mentor and seeker quickly intersects with similar journeys through other relationships. Small groups can help the seeker, of course. What about the mentor? Mentoring relationships underline the urgency for the mentor to receive mentoring. In order to help others grow spiritually, one must also grow spiritually. The mentor becomes the seeker, in need of the same leading questions, challenging assertions, decisive interventions, and pregnant silences as everyone else.

Walk with me. That simple invitation leads to a more complex journey. The timeline may be short, long, or intermittent. The challenges are sometimes predictable, and often surprising. The growth may accumulate slowly or come in spurts of maturity. The accumulating effect is personal confidence, deeper serenity, and clearer purpose. Christian mentoring may well use the language of pilgrimage, temptation, and discipline. The result is an acute sensitivity to incarnation, companionship with Christ, and courageous commitment to God's mission to redeem the world.

Snapshot

The person I will call "Dan" interrupted me while I was on coffee break at a large conference in which I was a minor speaker. An introvert I may be, but my intuition was that there was more behind his request that I autograph his book. So I closed my computer with an intentional snap, a clear signal that I was setting things aside and listening. It required only a few leading questions to learn that he was a former chemical engineer who had abandoned his career and staked the financial stability of his family to become a pastor-in-training. Now he had had three years of church life and had learned to hate every minute of it. His anger was palpable, but so also was his confusion about his true calling.

We established a six month covenant (that was eventually renewed three times ... and then a fourth time after a hiatus of a year). We agreed to an hour long, monthly webcam conversation, linked by unlimited email and occasional face-to-face meetings as travel permitted. If you glance ahead at the seven stages of mentoring discussed in the next chapter, you will better understand what I mean when I say that our conversations mainly focused on steps 2, 4, 5, and 6. Dan was pretty clear about his experience with Jesus Christ since he had been called to ministry after witnessing corporate injustices overseas, and he had had enough therapy and personality testing to know his strengths and weaknesses. However, he lacked spiritual discipline. He was constantly succumbing to manipulations and temptations, and obviously struggled with the misplaced or non-existent accountability of the local church. Where was he going? Should he quit parish ministry entirely? What did God want from him?

My goal here is to share something of the structure of our conversation ... or perhaps I should better say the path of opportunity in our dialogue. It took several sessions just to wade through the morass of his emotions, sort out the popcorn of his ideas, and help him accept that clarity about personal mission wasn't going to result from a strategic plan. Of course he didn't expect me to tell him what to do, but I think he did expect me to have a ready-made curriculum and guaranteed timeline.

Over the first six months, our conversation moved forward primarily through occasionally challenging assertions, and a lot of decisive interventions. The assertions helped us cut through the theological fog of compromises and conditions with which we surround faith. Yes, I really did believe God was fully present in the Eucharist. Did he? Yes, I really did believe the Apostles Creed. Did he? No, I didn't think every word of scripture was infallibly relevant to contemporary living. Did he? Yes, I was confident that Christ called every Christian to real ministry. Was he? We did not agree on everything, and that wasn't important. What was important was that he stopped playing games and staked his life, relationships, and livelihood on faith alone.

The interventions were more common, often unpredictable, and resulted in both painful confessions and joyous exultations. Dan had a lot of excess baggage, or "deadweight," that he was carrying around. He felt extraordinary guilt about his first failed marriage, was far too materialistic for his own good, gave up too quickly in the face of adversity, and repressed his anger at everything, to the point that he became chronically depressed. Among his "roadblocks" were the memories of abuse from the fundamentalist church of his childhood, and the fact that his children resented his career choice.

In his case, it was the "sidetracks" that were the most significant obstacles to meaning and purpose. He constantly wanted to talk about theology. If we got too close to discussing a real manipulation or temptation, Dan would want to debate creationism and theories of evolution. He also obsessed over "good worship," and was constantly worried that he might offend someone. Again and again he would choose the easy road of following some pet project, personal crusade, or clever idea, without ever pausing to align his decision with God's purpose to redeem the world, Christ's commandment to multiply disciples, or his own legacy that would make the world a better place.

In the latter months of our covenant, the "pregnant silences" grew longer. It's not that he was bored, or that we had run out of things to discuss, but that he was digesting a lot of new insights and sensing the seismic shifts that were taking place in his life. The last "pregnant silence" lasted for a year. When we reconnected again, he had finally jettisoned deadweights of material success, accepted God's acceptance of him, talked with his wife about past guilt, let go of his anger toward the church of his childhood, and was ready to surrender to God's will. Then we talked about personal mission and career choices. You might like to know that he left parish ministry to become CEO of a faith-based non-profit organization.

The Seven Stages of Mentoring

Imagine watching two people walking together in earnest conversation. Perhaps they are in a city park across the street, and you have the advantage of observation from a hotel window several stories up. It is noon when you first observe them, and they are still talking an hour later. Clearly they are using their lunch hour for this conversation. It must be pretty important. Around and around the park they go, sometimes sitting on a bench, then moving again. Occasionally their conversation is animated with arms and hands gesturing. One speaks, then the other speaks. Sometimes they stop abruptly, unmoving, listening intently. In our day of cellular communication, it is hard to imagine that one or the other's cell phone has rung several times, but they ignore it.

There are moments when the busy activity of the city intrudes on their conversation. Occasionally they step aside for another pedestrian, assist a child across the street, give a coin to a person in need, or even point to some object of interest, but they always return instantly to their conversation. Such concentration! Perched as you are in the window of your room, you may well wonder just how long this conversation has been going on. Perhaps they meet regularly like this every week. Perhaps the park is an exception, and they normally talk over lunch in some café. Perhaps they carry on the conversation through email and text messages when they are apart.

Mostly you wonder what on earth they are talking about. It could be about any acute crisis, or common interest, but *perhaps* you are really witnessing a mentoring conversation. If one of the people was a priest, you might deduce from his or her clothes that a *Christian* mentoring conversation was taking place, but in the absence of such telltale signs you might still speculate that something spiritual was unfolding. Spirituality is in the air of post-modern living, and even the secularity of modern times has been infused and transformed because of it. More people are wondering about God, seeking the touch of the Holy, and trying to figure out how to connect their desperate lives with God's higher purpose than ever before. Indeed, they are more likely *not* to have mentoring conversations with the priest because the representatives of religious institutions are regarded as having mixed motivations at best. An authentic lay person or spiritually alive, ordinary pilgrim like you will be sufficient.

I hope that by now I have made my point that mentoring is *purposefully messy*. There is a purpose to it. Mentor and seeker yearn to experience God, live in companionship with Christ, and find their place in God's plan for the world. The journey to get there, however, is very messy. The style of the mentor in asking leading questions, making challenging assertions, intervening in decisive ways, and welcoming pregnant silences is that of an innovative musician or dancer rather than a methodical researcher or lecturer. Mentoring is messy. Steps forward, steps backward, steps to the side, twists, turns, leaps, and pirouettes ... the mentor seems to be moving to music that the seeker can't quite hear yet. Even the mentor is not quite sure what the next move will look like. Life is messy, figuring life out is messy, and the Holy Spirit shaping life is messy.

It is also true that mentoring is *messily purposeful*. There is a discernible pattern to mentoring. However messy the journey might be, once you look back and examine it, there is a sensible flow to the process. It may be misleading to describe this flow in *stages* of mentoring, because that might imply some linear curriculum from "introductory" to "advanced" mentoring that would resemble a program rather than a relationship. One does not complete an oral exam for "Christian Experience 101" and then register for "Christian Experience 201." It might be better to say that mentoring proceeds from crisis to crisis, or from breakthrough to breakthrough. Each "stage" is marked by stress and stress release, consternation and discovery, or discomfort and serenity. A breakthrough in spiritual growth might move the seeker into brand new territory, or unexpectedly return the seeker to revisit previous territory, but overall there is a discernible progress to be made. The goal, after all, is to discern personal mission or calling, and until that becomes clearer we remain restless for more.

Return to those two people you observed walking around and around the park over the lunch hour. You know what it *looks like* from the relative safety of your hotel window, but what does it *feel like* for the two people below?

If the people walking below are actually in the midst of a mentoring relationship, it probably doesn't *feel like* a walk in the park. It feels like white-water rafting down the Colorado River in early spring. If you could monitor their blood pressure, heart rate, and the dilation of their eyes, even their physiological reactions would not really be appropriate for what we would normally expect of a walk in the park. Both the seeker *and the mentor* feel the exhilaration and panic of a barely controllable ride down the river. Sometimes they feel in control of the situation: seeker paddling, mentor steering, making sense of the scenery, and making progress as they journey down the river. They intentionally glide by this rock, struggle over that sandbar, and catch their breath in some quiet pool. Sometimes they feel quite out of control: paddles lost, steering gone, scenery a blur, and under water as much as on top of it. They are swept away by the Spirit, crashing into rocks, carried away by rapids, and spinning in whirlpools.

This is why before they even begin the walk, or start the journey, or launch the board (choose your metaphor) the mentor always warns the seeker that this *will not be a walk in the park!* It may look like a walk in the park. Outside observers might even envy the conversations if they happen to watch from the safety of their office cubicle or suburban home, but it will not feel like a walk in the park. It will feel quite different. If you want to embark on a mentoring relationship, then be prepared for an unpredictable process of change. Don't count on ending up in the same career, or with the same pattern of intimate friends, or with the same lifestyle habits, or with the same income and stability and accoutrements of living as when you started. It *may* be with you at the end, or it *may* be lost overboard along the way. We just don't know.

The Seven Stages

Every mentoring relationship is different. Each person grows at their own pace, and in their own order, largely dependent on their personal sense of urgency, the attention of the mentor, and the work of the Holy Spirit. Mentors tend to be opportunists, rather than planners. They are driven by flashes of insight, rather than agendas. Yet they do set out with a plan. Spiritual growth tends to be marked by seven breakthrough experiences.

Step 1:
Connect the seeker with his or her own,
intimate experience of Christ

The very first step is to share with the seeker the *story* of Christ. One of the huge shifts to the post-modern world is that today most people simply do not know the basic story of Jesus. Who is he? Where did he come from? How was he born? What did he do? What did he teach? Who were his friends? Where did he live? Where did he go? What happened to him in the end? Our situation today is quite similar to the ancient world. It is a bubbling cauldron of spirituality, of myth and misconception, of yearning and prejudice, and of misinformation and miscommunication. In order to talk about incarnation, or God-with-us, people have to be familiar with the basic story of Jesus.

Paul and Peter may have told the basic story of Jesus in their preaching, but it didn't take the ancient Christians long to realize they needed to publish a basic story. The Gospel of Mark is reputed to be the first, and simplest, attempt to lay out the bare facts. Then the earliest church realized that the story of Jesus was tied to a larger story of Israel. In order to understand Jesus' story, you need to understand Israel's story. To fill this need, the Gospel of Matthew begins with a genealogy, and connects the teachings of Jesus to the Old Testament. Then the earliest church realized that the story of Jesus was also tied to a history of God's redemption for the world, so the Gospel of Luke became chapter one of the Acts of the Apostles, and connects Jesus with God's cross-cultural blessing. Finally, the earliest church realized that the story of Jesus was further tied to a fundamental fracture and healing of existence, so the Gospel of John connects Jesus with the final resolution of the problem of evil.

There are literally lifetimes of reflection about the story of Jesus contained in just four Gospels. The mentoring relationship does not have time to accomplish that much. The trouble is that most seekers know almost nothing about the story of Jesus in the first place. Even if they think they know something, it is often piecemeal, distorted by prejudice, warped by ecclesiastical dogmas, or infused with other mythologies. Ignorance of the story of Jesus is really only part of a greater post-modern ignorance of the history of events and ideas *in general*. As the liberal arts have been displaced by specialized professional education in business and sciences, most Americans don't know the story of Abraham Lincoln either. Of course, one can experience the immediacy of God without the story of Abraham Lincoln, but Christians believe it is nearly impossible to do so without the story of Jesus.

The first step of Christian mentoring is to tell the story of Jesus. Imitate the earliest Christians, however. Tell it *in your own words*. Reading it is very helpful. Telling it in your own words is even more helpful. You may fear that telling the story in your own words might somehow skew the story. Your telling of the story might color the story. You might emphasize certain things, forget other things, get something in the wrong chronological order, or quote something in the wrong way. You will double check your memory against the four Gospels. In the end, you have to tell the story in your own words, because that is what the Gospel writers did themselves. They, too, double-checked their story-telling against the memory of the living apostles, but they told the story in their own words, which is why the stories of the four Gospels are the same and yet different.

When you tell the Jesus story in your own words, his story intersects with the story of your life, and it is precisely that honesty which is the foundation of all mentoring conversations. It is *your* telling of the story. It is not Matthew's, Mark's, Luke's, or John's telling of the story that ultimately counts. The seeker wants to know about how your life has intersected with Jesus' life in profound and blessed ways. The seeker has come to you because of your *life*, and not because of your *knowledge*. He or she is not that interested in your interpretation of what Matthew, Mark, Luke, or John said. They are interested in what *you* say. If the story of Jesus matters at all, it is because that story has changed *your life* for the better. That interaction or intersection of Jesus' story with your story is the beginning of all mentoring conversations. It is your *experience* with Jesus that matters.

The springboard to conversation may be how your life story intersects with the story of Jesus, but the goal of the conversation is to help the seeker uncover or discover how his or her own life story intersects with the story of Jesus. It is really not about you, but about the seeker. Part of your blessing is that you want others to blessed — not necessarily in the same way as it happened for you, but in some way that blesses the other.

Mentoring conversations move on to unpack the life story of the seeker. This is not psychotherapy (although therapy can be helpful), and the mentor is not a psychotherapist. The mentor helps the seeker explore his or her story. The questions are not unlike the basic questions about Jesus. Who are you? Where did you come from? How were you born? What have you done? What do you say? Who are your friends? Where have you lived? Where have you gone? What will happen to you in the end? Mentor and seeker are looking for ways in which their life stories have intersected with the story of Jesus.

Talk about intersections between one's life and the story of Jesus is grounded in a key assumption. This is a conviction for the mentor, and perhaps only an intuition for the seeker. The assumption is that God has not just begun to mess with your life today. God has been messing with your life since the moment you were conceived. You may not have known it, and perhaps only recently have you become vaguely and disturbingly aware of it. You may have recognized God's nearness, and later forgotten, doubted, or rejected it. You may not remember anything remotely like God's nearness. Mentoring conversations begin with the assumption, however, that God has been "incarnate" in your personal existence from the very beginning.

- **Meetings:**

  The intersections of one's life and Jesus' story may have been just occasional meetings. They may have seemed like chance encounters on the road, brief moments when you were touched by the Holy, and then they passed. When asked about spiritual experiences, people often recount mountain views and ocean vistas, natural beauty, childbirth, intimate attachments, homecomings, and other moments when time seemed to stand still.

  The trouble is that it is difficult to distinguish sentimentality from spirituality. Once sentimentality sours, it turns to resentment. People try to recapture a moment and are angered when it is impossible. If the moment is *spiritual*, rather than just sentimental, people try to recover the reality behind the moment rather than the moment itself. Mentoring is not interested in nostalgia. Mentoring uses these experiences as gateways to explore deeper meaning and significance. The conversation between Jesus and the Samaritan woman at the well models this kind of discernment (John 4).

- **Mergers:**

  The intersections of one's life and Jesus' story may have been mergers that reshaped, reversed, or restored life forever. They may be described in "lost and found" or "before and after" metaphors. When asked about spiritual experiences, people often reveal turning points in their lives: conversions, remarriages, vocational changes, migrations, and other occasions when time seemed to accelerate.

  The trouble is that it is difficult to distinguish between self-congratulation, good luck, and God's expectation. Once progress slows down, it turns to cynicism. What they thought to be true, people conclude was a lie. Leaders are hypocrites and they are victims of a conspiracy. Mentoring is not interested in explaining the motives of others or proving the existence of God. Mentoring uses these experiences to reveal the movement of the Spirit and to explore the original intentions of God. The conversation between

Jesus and Thomas models this kind of guidance (John 11:16, 14:5, and 20:24-29).

- **Collisions:**

    The intersections of one's life and Jesus' story may have been collisions that disrupted, shattered, or challenged attitudes, behavior patterns, or lifestyles. They may be described as breakdowns or crises that temporarily or permanently changed one's life forever. People do not often associate these catastrophes with spiritual experiences, and yet the repercussions have both deepened or curtailed their faith. Accidents, disease, divorce, unemployment, homelessness, and death are occasions when time seems to fracture into a meaningless series of ticks and tocks.

    The trouble is that it is difficult to distinguish between personal responsibility, bad luck, and mysterious purpose. Once stability is lost, people turn to recrimination. People blame themselves or just curse their fate. Mentoring is not interested in placing blame or perpetuating self-pity. Mentoring uses these experiences to access God's mystery and discover new hope. The conversation between Jesus, Mary and Martha, and the death and raising of Lazarus, models this kind of encouragement.

A synonym for "intersection" is the word "crossroad." Aside from the literal meaning that the story of the mentor and the story of the seeker are intersecting, there is an obvious nuance that the story of Jesus is intersecting with both. The seeker would not be in the conversation at all unless he or she felt that his or her life was "at a crossroads," and it is the Christian mentor who helps interpret this by adding the third intersection with the story of Jesus.

The *story* of Jesus leads to the *experience* of Christ. According to the apostle Paul (or the anonymous disciple he mentored), *in Jesus the fullness of God dwells bodily* (Col. 2:9). Jesus is the intersection of the infinite and the finite. The name change to Jesus *Christ* more accurately describes his paradoxical identity. The goal of mentoring, however, is not primarily to explore the philosophical or theological arguments for this Christian faith. Instead, the goal of mentoring is to explore the existential implications for this Christian faith. God is with us. What does that mean here, now, in the particularity of my life, and your life, and the life of that homeless person disappearing around the corner?

Seekers are seeking the immanence of God. They look for the fullness of God, fully experienced, as God is inclined to connect with their peculiarly small and paradoxically important lives. There are two reasons why the institutional church, with all its programs and liturgies, is deemed irrelevant by seekers.

1) The institutional church filters the glory of God through layers upon layers of rationalized traditions. It is like a parent admonishing a child never to look directly at the sun, and then manufacturing ever darker sunglasses and ever thicker suntan lotions to avoid God's startling power.

2) The institutional church breaks the power of God into little, consumable pieces. It is like a corporation that doesn't want to give it all away in a single sale. Buy the basic package, and then each additional experience of grace will require an additional sacrifice.

Seekers, however, are eager to experience the whole thing. Of course, it may be harder to do than they anticipate. It may have implications that they can't imagine. Experiencing God incarnate may blow them away, overturn their ship, and wash them ashore on a different career path, in a different location, with different companions, and nothing but the clothes on their back, *but that is OK!* Such is the starvation post-modern people feel after a steady diet of secular modernity.

Mentors help seekers rediscover, or discover for the first time, the fullness of God in Christ. Mentors are convinced that Jesus is the Christ. If they have any doubts or reservations about this, they cannot be mentors. Mentors do not claim to know everything about the mystery of incarnation, and they may even acknowledge how little they actually do know about the mystery of incarnation, but they never doubt the incarnation. This conviction is *not* grounded in philosophical arguments or theological education. It is *not* grounded in historical traditions or in their confidence in the written record of scripture. It is grounded in their own experience of Christ.

I cannot stress enough that mentoring is not about theological education. It is about baring one's soul — making oneself vulnerable to laughter, abuse, or martyrdom — by sharing what God through Christ has done to change one's life. Mentors *are convinced* that Jesus is the Christ because they *have met* Jesus the Christ. Like Paul, mentors can say, "last of all, as to one untimely born, he appeared to me" (1 Cor. 15:9). Mentors are not convinced by words, but by experience. That is exactly what they help seekers to do: experience the fullness of God in the here and now of their lives.

How does one even talk about so great a mystery? The fullness of God intersects with a puny life. That God should bother to intersect with one's life story at all is fantastical. I first described the six basic ways people experience Christ in my book *Talisman: Global Positioning for the Soul*.[9] The spiritual disciplines there are considerably more advanced than what occurs at first in Christian mentoring. These six ways, however, help mentors guide seekers to reflect on their life journeys as they intersect with Christ.

Begin by guiding the seeker to understand his or her personal search in six ways. We are motivated to seek God because, at different times, with different intensities, we are:

- ✓ **broken** ... and searching for healing;
- ✓ **lost** ... and searching for guidance;
- ✓ **lonely** ... and searching for lasting intimacy;
- ✓ **anxious** ... and searching for hope;
- ✓ **victimized** ... and searching for justice; and
- ✓ **trapped** ... and searching for liberation.

One or two of these yearnings may be acute at any given time. The others are latent, but still present. Some may be chronic conditions. However, these six experiences are the very stuff of existence. Starting from our first wail when we are born, and ending with our last breath when we die, and however many seconds and moments lie in between, this is what shapes our existence. We may temporarily avoid these six yearnings by affluence, good luck, or simple denial, but our mortality will always break through.

The mentor asks: How have you experienced these yearnings in your own life story? How did you try to solve them? How long did your solutions last?

The six experiences of Christ are the specific ways God incarnate addresses each of these six yearnings. Again, we may experience this grace at different times, with different intensities, but these are the six basic ways people experience God in the midst of the life struggle that is existence.

---

[9] *Talisman: Global Positioning for the Soul* (Chalice Press, 2006).

- ❖ **The Healer** … restores wholeness
- ❖ **The Guide** … shows the way
- ❖ **The Perfect Human** … provides true intimacy
- ❖ **The Promise Keeper** … gives hope for tomorrow
- ❖ **The Vindicator** … brings justice
- ❖ **The Liberator** … rescues us from our addictions

Incarnation is the intersection of spiritual yearning and divine grace. Human beings "reach up," which means that we reach beyond ourselves, and God "reaches down," which means that the divine enters our personal life history.

My daughter drew this picture as a child. I first used this picture in my book *Talisman: Global Positioning for the Soul.* It expresses the manner in which we experience, however fleetingly, the real presence of God.

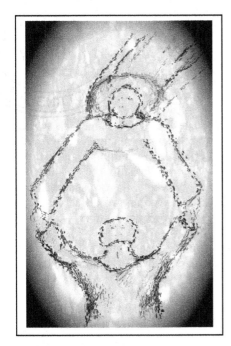

Help the seeker start with his or her memories of spiritual yearning, and then explore if, when, and how that yearning was addressed by God. That intersection may not be an "embrace." Perhaps it was only a touch of the fingertips, a brush with the Holy, or a fragrance of hope. Build on this to expand the awareness of the seeker of the immanence of God in his or her own personal history.

This picture is deliberately unsophisticated, unprofessional, and perhaps even "child-like" in its presentation. That is how seekers begin to awaken their sensitivity to "God-with-us." It may be a memory forgotten, or a hope never really explored, or a redemption never fully appreciated. The very fact of survival means that the seeker is *still here*, and *still seeking*. This in itself reveals the intuition that there is something more to life that is yet to come.

Whatever it is, mentors help seekers "prize out" this pearl of greatest worth and reset this gem as the centerpiece of their lives. It becomes a reference point for all the mentoring to come, and provides a source of self-esteem that allows the seeker to endure future frustration with patience and persistence. The seeker is like a merchant who searches for a pearl of surpassing worth, and once he has found it, sells all that he has to buy that pearl (Matt. 13:45-46).

The experience of Jesus Christ as fully divine and fully human, infinite mystery, and crucial for salvation (the ancient confession of Chalcedon) is not a theological statement but an existential sigh of seekers everywhere.

This single step alone may occupy the entire attention of mentor and seeker for a considerable time ... even for a lifetime. However, at some point the mentor will sense that progress is stalled, going in circles, or just "spinning its wheels." There needs to be a plan, strategy, or discipline to continue the search. The seeker is like the woman who has lost a coin, and cleans the house diligently until she finds it (Luke 14:8-9). At first the housekeeper searches for the lost coin by frantically tossing things about. Then she finally decides to conduct the search methodically. What began as a search has become a quest. The search may take a long time, or perhaps a lifetime, but the housekeeper is determined to find it.

Snapshot

Sometimes in order to get to the heart of the matter, we have to start with a presenting problem. My mentoring relationship with B. began in seminary, and drifted off and on over the years ... sometime informally and sometimes formally, with occasional gaps of non-communication. In fact, it was this very lack of self-discipline that was part of the problem that just kept getting worse and worse for B. His approach/avoidance attitude toward the institutional church eventually led him to a crisis over his vocation.

Did B. really want to stay in professional ministry or not? The list of things he didn't like about the church was long. The list of things that kept him in the ministry was getting shorter and shorter. The easiest course was for him to gripe a lot, project a sardonic attitude in denominational meetings, and deliberately act outrageously on Mondays and piously the rest of the week. The one thing he couldn't seem to do was be decisive. "Are you in or are you out?" He couldn't decide. Finally, his third wife had had it. His marriage was again on the line because deep inside he really didn't know what God wanted to do with his life.

B. was like an increasing number of ministers and priests that I know. The career that seemed attractively stable and counter-cultural in the 70's has turned out to be unstable and nonsensical in the millennium. I observed B. actually working his way *backwards* through the mentoring process. Unable to define his personal mission in life, he tried dedicating himself to the institutional church. He served as a middle judicatory leader and completed a D. Min. degree in preaching. The end of B.'s second marriage led him to confront his alcohol addiction and reexamine his personal life. Then he immersed himself in human potential therapies to explore his personality type, Enneagram, and spiritual gifts profile. He flirted with Celtic spirituality for a few years, and spent a sabbatical and two vacations in various monasteries in Scotland and the United States.

B. and I reconnected during a lecture series in Nova Scotia. I had (once again) asked the group "What is it about your experience with Jesus that this community cannot live without?" Several men and women had shared their testimony with profound modesty and joy, but B. had come to the microphone in tears. "I've been a church leader for thirty years," he said, "and still don't have an answer to that question." It was a heart-wrenching admission, but finally, after all this time, he had come to the heart of the matter. He had explored all of the steps of Christian maturity, but because he never really resolved the very first step, his entire journey had been fruitless. Now, finally, he wanted to *know* Jesus Christ, and was willing to stake his entire life on the outcome of that relationship.

The best way for him to meet Jesus was to become immersed in mission. Leave the security of pulpit and manse, stop thinking about self, and pay complete attention to strangers who are desperately in need of grace. Our mentoring unfolded through email and phone calls as he invested himself more and more in the sufferings of others. Gradually he stopped worrying about Christian liturgy and protecting "good worship." he stopped complaining about poor stewardship and insufficient salaries. He forgot to care about protecting his day off. He and his wife sold their house, survived on monthly leases, and traveled from one disaster zone to another, finding ways to bless strangers in trouble. Once he stopped looking for love, B. fell in love. Once he stopped trying to find *his* relationship with Jesus, Jesus forged a relationship with him. His experience of Jesus was that of the Promise Keeper and the Hope Bringer, and that is what eventually led him to find himself and discern his life purpose in a series of non-profit emergency relief programs and para-church projects. It not only transformed his life, but it saved his marriage. He was really *happy* for the first time in his life.

Step 2:
Guide the seeker to develop spiritual habits for daily living

At some point in the process of mentoring, and often as a kind of "second step" to the recovery of Christ experiences, the seekers must develop spiritual habits for daily living. I prefer the word "habit" to the traditional term "discipline" primarily because the former is readily familiar to the seeker, while the latter is foreign and intimidating to modern ears. "Habits" are behavior patterns that are often unconscious until they are broken, whereupon the individual does not feel "normal" and has an inner compulsion to restore those habits.

Spiritual practices are good habits, not unlike personal hygiene, proper diet, regular physical exercise, and mental acuity. Indeed, spiritual habits may embrace all of these as well. The enemy of all "good habits" is "temptation." People are constantly lured to replace good habits with bad, or to abandon "habit" entirely to live solely for the moment. This is not only the predicament for seekers, but also for mentors, and indeed for every creature existing. Temptation is as natural as self-centeredness, and so long as ego (self-gratification, self-aggrandizement, and even self-reliance) is dominant, spiritual habits will be hard to maintain. Since "individualization" is the hallmark of modernity, habits of any kind are hard to maintain, and post-modern people know it. While they may be skeptical of absolutes, post-modern people are remarkably keen to protect good habits of physical, emotional, relational, mental, and yes, spiritual fitness. Talk about good habits and people know what you mean.

If temptation is so pervasive, it is "tempting" to objectify "temptation" in a "tempter." This is a major roadblock to mentoring spiritual habits, and holds seekers back from the hard work of developing spiritual practices. The objectification of temptation may be to blame society, public education, capitalism, genetics, or some other devil that "makes me do it," but the point of doing so is always to escape personal responsibility. Spiritual habits, like all habits, are a personal responsibility. There is no power to blame other than you, even though the power to change comes from beyond yourself.

Developing spiritual habits without some reference to the experience of Christ is like trying to learn to swim without first learning to breathe. Like Paul, the good we desire to do we fail to accomplish, and the bad we want to avoid we end up doing (Rom. 7:14-25). The only way not to feel wretched about our struggle with temptation is to return to the central experience of Christ and start over again.

The basic shape of spiritual habit has been modeled by historic Christian figures, and is taught in many growing churches. Of course, it may be easy to describe but difficult to do.

Daily Habits

- Prayer: Rotating among intercession, supplication, and thanksgiving
- Bible: Reading or studying scripture in an intentional pattern
- Listening: Conversing with other seekers and prayerful interaction with culture

The greatest difficulty for daily spiritual habits lies in conversing with other seekers and interacting with culture. We often imagine that Christians beyond North America, particularly in totalitarian or former communist cultures, must surely have the most difficulty talking about Christ in everyday conversation, demonstrating public piety, and interacting with the political, educational, economic, and communication systems of culture. It is a shock to realize that North America is increasingly hostile to disciplined Christian living.

The value of the church in the west (from the point of view of the systems of culture) lies in socialization. If Christians contribute to the overall process of assimilation into the policies, philosophies, consumerism, and language, they are protected and rewarded. Christian piety *as an instrument of propaganda* is generally acceptable provided it is "kept in its place." However, that appropriate "place" for Christian lifestyle is increasingly restricted. It is a matter of convenience in politics, curiosity or denigration in education, laughable in economics, and dangerous in communication. Just try to exercise daily habits of conversation with seekers, and intentional Christian interaction with the system of culture in the manner of Christians, even at the beginning of the 20th century, and you risk negative consequences.

Daily spiritual habits today, in western culture, are far more risky than for many Christians beyond North America. It is not that Christians will be imprisoned or killed, but in a thousand ways they will be gradually ostracized and marginalized. Promotions will be harder to get, elections will be harder to win (especially local elections), teaching positions will be harder to achieve, and positive press will be harder to find. Daily spiritual habit is the most threatening, unsettling, counter-cultural thing anyone can do.

Mentors in conversation with seekers will encounter considerable resistance to the idea of *daily* spiritual habits, and in particular to the habit of public conversation and cultural interaction. People know they risk neighborhood friendships, family harmony, promotions at work, and status in service clubs. They fear post-moderns will treat them the way moderns treated the Amish. At best they will be perceived as curiously dressed, peculiarly old-fashioned, and acceptable so long as they stay on the farm. At worst they will be perceived as judgmental, exclusive, and threatening if they should ever be given real power.

Given the risks of obvious Christianity in the increasingly hostile western environment, seekers will always opt to privatize religion. Daily prayer and daily Bible reading are fine so long as they can be done in relative isolation from culture. Mentors need to insist on the public nature of Christian behavior. This does *not* mean that seekers must hand out tracts on street corners, shout scripture verses in the food court, or interrupt conversation in the coffee house with accusatory questions like "Are you saved?" After all, that's not *conversation*.

Mentors guide seekers best when they literally apprentice them in this daily spiritual habit. Take them along and model the practice. The best conversation is about 2/3 listening, and 1/3 talking. It does not intrude on people, but builds respectful relationships with people. It is alert to every opportunity to exercise Christian virtues, and is ready with a simple, direct explanation if that behavior is ever questioned. Conversation is authentic when it is consistent with a larger behavioral matrix, which for Christians is a matrix of love, joy, peace, patience, kindness, gentleness, generosity, fidelity, and self-control. This is inevitably counter-cultural, because most conversation today arises from a matrix of anger, jealousy, envy, competition, licentiousness, idolatry, and self-absorption.

Christian conversation may become "prophetic," because the matrix of Christian behavior invariably leads to the protection of human rights (just as the matrix of most contemporary conversation leads invariably to indifference to human rights). The daily spiritual habit may become a springboard to advocacy, intervention, or other risky activities. The intentional exercise of daily spiritual habits makes it almost impossible for a Christian to observe injustice and not do something about it.

Seekers quickly realize that *daily* spiritual habits require stamina. Mentors therefore encourage them to maintain *weekly* spiritual habits so that they can keep going on a daily basis.

Weekly Habits

❖ Small Group: Participate in the small group that addresses the point of your need
❖ Mission Service: Participate in the mission team that focuses your compassion for others
❖ Worship: Participate in corporate worship relevant to your lifestyle and yearnings

The greatest difficulty for weekly spiritual habits lies, perhaps surprisingly, in regular corporate worship. We often imagine that this will be the easiest part, but rapidly declining worship attendance in every denomination or established church reveals evidence to the contrary. People generally don't want to attend corporate worship every week. Seekers are generally much more willing to participate in a small group or mission service. Both are familiar and rewarding. The small group is a bond of friendship; the mission service brings the satisfaction of philanthropy. In a world of 12 step programs and non-profit agencies, these are culturally acceptable. Why will seekers resist going to church?

Mentors need to address the real issue. Seekers will immediately argue that they have no time, and complain about work schedules, family time, amateur sports for their children, and so on. Mentors know that time is not the real issue, since people will make time for what is important. Seekers will also argue that worship is boring, and there is no opportunity to worship in the styles with which they are familiar. Mentors know that style is not the real issue, since people get bored with anything before long.

Mentors know that the real issue is *relevance*. Seekers do not go to corporate worship because they can't find a church that focuses worship on their real life situations and spiritual yearnings. There are six kinds of yearning, six experiences of Christ, and six basic kinds of worship:

Worship ...	brings people to Christ ...	through experiences of grace.
Coaching Worship	Jesus the Spiritual Guide	Encouraging Relationships
Celebration Worship	Jesus the Promise Keeper	Hopeful Attitudes
Care-Giving Worship	Jesus the Healer	Healthy Living
Transforming Worship	Christ the Liberator	Fresh Start
Educational Worship	Christ the Perfect Human	Truth about Life
Missional Worship	Christ the Vindicator	Acceptance and Justice

The problem is that much corporate worship is merely blended, trying to do everything and succeeding at nothing. Or worship is liturgically standardized, following a Christian year or a common lectionary that few understand, and established by unknown authorities nobody respects. Or worship is simply stylized, appealing to aesthetic taste while indifferent to spiritual thirst.

Mentors are in the uncomfortable position of knowing that corporate worship is crucial to sustain daily spiritual habits, but unable to send the seeker to any relevant worship service. Literally hundreds of churches are within driving distance of the seeker, but none of them are relevant. They generally compete with each other to attract a diminishing number of culturally acceptable Christians, but seem incapable of attracting a growing number of counter-cultural Christians.

Mentors may shape corporate worship themselves to be relevant to the spiritual thirst of seekers. They do it, however, not as preachers or liturgists or career church pastors, but as simple mentors trying to provide weekly worship to sustain daily discipline. In short, these mentors become the post-modern abbots and priors of the post-modern monastic community.

It is more likely that mentors will simple search diligently until they can find a weekly corporate worship that is actually relevant to the seeker. That may take some searching, but today it may be rewarded. Church plants, house churches, and other transformed Christian communities may provide the relevance seekers seek. Mentors will know from experience, however, to monitor relevance closely. House churches come and go, and all too many shape themselves around the needs of a few. New churches tend to become self-centered ecclesiastical institutions after the first five years.

If mentors have drawn seekers this far into spiritual habits, it becomes clear that *daily* and *weekly* spiritual disciplines are not enough to sustain a *lifestyle* that is distinctively Christian. In a sense, the peak of success from daily and weekly spiritual habits is that a Christian will become a *knowledgeable tither*. A Christian lifestyle demands more. It is too easy for unexplainable evil, tragedy, or injustice to undermine a spiritual life based solely on daily and weekly habits.

Monthly or Ongoing Habits

❖ Journal: Creating and reviewing a personal log of one's spiritual quest
❖ Talisman: Focusing on an evocative object, song, or image
❖ Accountability: Intentional self-examination with trusted companions

The greatest difficulty for ongoing spiritual habits lies in accountability. Journaling is a fairly common practice in an era of record keeping, text messaging, and dictation software. The use of talismans as reminders or evocative objects to focus hope and guide meditation is increasingly familiar in the omni-literate, image rich, and sound-byte driven post-modern world. Accountability, however, comes hard.

The mentoring relationship itself provides such accountability, but it takes time to build that trust. The initial conversations between seeker and mentor are earnest, but not particularly assertive. It takes time, usually through the coaching of daily and weekly spiritual habits, before either seeker or mentor is ready to accept such responsibility. Real trust only emerges after it is tested by life struggles and rewarded by spiritual victories.

The greater challenge is to relocate accountability beyond the mentoring relationship itself. The ancient Christian precedent is the "Pilgrim Band" or the "Holy Order." The military model is the "band of brothers." The closest contemporary experience (more myth than reality) is the community of "friends." These are all close communities of intentional accountability. They help people grow with practical training, opportunities for repentance, and communal insight.

Mentors may not be able to create such communities of accountability for the seeker, but they can help the seeker do this for him or herself. The cornerstone for such communities is that they are about survival and destination. The pilgrim band, for example, exists so that traveling companions can defend themselves from the perils of the road, and so that each participant can arrive at a holy destination. There is much that is associated with Christian institutions that is non-essential for the pilgrim band: good feelings, mutual friendliness, agreement about doctrine, shared stylistic appreciation, common enthusiasm to protect a heritage, similar views on public policy, and many other things are *not* essential, and even act as *potential sidetracks*, from the real purpose of accountability.

The kind of accountability necessary for the mentoring relationship focuses specifically on survival and destination. The members of a community of accountability help one another resist temptation, avoid manipulation, and overcome persecution by remaining unswervingly loyal to the experience of Christ. And they assist one another to make whatever sacrifices are necessary to arrive at the destination that is their hope in Christ.

Mentors need to be clear about the point of practicing spiritual habits. Mentoring began with the experience of Christ. Helping seekers shape spiritual habits is the means to explore the mystery of incarnation. That is the point ... and the only point ... for spiritual habits. The practice makes us more alert to God-with-us, more persistent even when we do not feel God-with-us, more prepared for the counter-cultural behavior that is demanded by God-with-us, and more courageous when God-with-us exposes us to criticism or abuse. Companionship with Christ is risky business.

Nowadays it is fashionable not only to compare, but to equate, physical and mental fitness with spiritual discipline. A quick walk through the book store sections for spirituality, holistic health, and well-being reveals how popular supposedly "spiritual habits" have become among aging boomers and restless post-moderns. However, the goals are not the same. These books encourage spiritual habits in order to explore *your soul* (i.e. human potential, ego, and the many facets of your personality). Their goal is to help you live a longer, happier, healthier life. Spiritual habits fit neatly with diet, exercise, enhancements for more satisfying sexuality, and financial planning, all with the goal of achieving a balanced life.

The goal for Christian spirituality is not the exploration of the human soul, but the mystery of Christ. The measure of success is not balanced living, but faithful living. Christian spiritual habits *may* help the individual focus energy, learn more, and avoid disease and depression. They *may* lead to a long life and balanced lifestyle, but they may also lead to a shorter life and an unbalanced lifestyle. Christian spiritual habits may actually sacrifice physical, mental, and relational well-being for a higher purpose. They may not lead to inner peace or financial success. They may lead to personal hardship and martyrdom. Companionship with Christ is risky business. Unity with Christ is worth it.

Snapshot

Interestingly enough, the people who seem most interested in developing spiritual habits in my current experience are multi-tasking, multi-media, techno-savvy 20-somethings. I wonder sometimes if this is because more and more youth seem to be diagnosed ADHD personalities, but I think it has more to do with reaching a critical mass of overload. There comes a point when life is just too complicated, and we are compelled to simplify. There are just too many text messages, facebook friends, external demands, daily personal crises, and ambiguous decisions than any given smart-phone-enhanced human being can manage.

This, at least, was the case for the young couple I met as part of a regional church planting initiative. They participated in a "House Church" made up of the lifestyle segment known as "Unattached Multi-Cultures." This segment was made up of highly mobile, multi-ethnic singles, single parents, and unmarried couples living in low-income downtown urban neighborhoods. The couple could describe with deep emotion their experience with Jesus Christ that had changed their lives ... but they couldn't seem to focus any continuing methodology to explore the significance of that experience for the future. The usual spiritual disciplines of Christendom (Bible studies, devotional prayers, weekly worship, small group meetings, journals and the like) were just too abstract, tedious, and boring. These individuals had the attention spans of gnats, but carried burdens of expectation the size of elephants.

Initially, we chucked all the usual devotional expectations associated with "spiritual discipline." I urged them to simply practice a discipline of remembering faces and praying for strangers. Every day (and sometimes at intervals throughout the day), they would rerun the data stream, starting with the present moment and working backwards. They would simply remember the image of each human being that had somehow attracted their attention, however fleetingly, whether positively or negatively, during the preceding hours. They would imagine the one thing that that person might need most, and pray for their blessing.

It soon became apparent that they needed help to concentrate on anything for over three minutes. I encouraged them each to select a talisman (devotional object) that automatically triggered God-sized feelings in their heart whenever they looked at it, listened to it, smelled it, stroked it, or tasted it. That would be the device on which to replay the images of intercessory prayer.

The more we prayed to bless strangers, the more strangers we began to notice who required a blessing, and the more time-consuming it became to rerun the videotape of the day. So we introduced the filter of six basic spiritual needs. We focused on each one in turn, and recalled images of people we had encountered who we instinctively categorized as broken, lost, lonely, anxious, victimized, or afraid. That readily led us to imagine Jesus the healer, guide, friend, encourager, vindicator, and transformer blessing them in new ways.

It took awhile, but in the end it was this Christocentrism that finally motivated the young couple to read their bible. The Bible became a book of blessings ... not a book of history, theology, future prediction, or institutional religion. This young couple became interested in blessings: blessing others, being blessed by others, and blessings in general. They read the Bible to discover more about grace.

Dialogue in the House Church became richer and deeper. New experiences of Jesus Christ were being revealed unexpectedly, in unlikely places with unusual people, on a daily basis. It was like being a part of a reality TV show in which the Holy Spirit was the principle protagonist. Once the day became an adventure, rather than a grind, spiritual discipline took on a whole new purpose. It wasn't about learning what happened back then, but interpreting what just happened here and now.

I don't think they will ever get into daily devotionals and journaling. They might read the newspaper with fresh eyes, blog, or post to U-Tube.

Step 3:
Guide the seeker to explore
his or her authenticity as a human being

The exercise of spiritual habits eventually takes the mentoring relationship to a new level. Once again I remind you that the mentoring process is intentional, but messy, and considerable time may be spent simply developing and maintaining spiritual habits. At some point, however, the seeker becomes intensely aware that companionship with Christ is very personal. Spiritual habits have made "God-with-us" as intimate as "God-with-me."

Spiritual habits cannot be standardized. What works for the mentor won't be as effective for the seeker. What works for one person may not work for another. Spiritual habits need to be customized to fit the unique personality and spiritual gifts of the individual. The mystery of Christ demands exploration of the mystery of me. If Christ is the perfection of what it means to be human, I cannot help but contrast that with my own imperfection as an example of humanity.

This step in the mentoring relationship usually begins simply enough as seekers try to customize spiritual practices to fit their lifestyles. There is an obvious "art" to a spiritually disciplined life lived under the conditions of culture.

- On the one hand, spiritual practices ought to shape lifestyle. They need to be uncomfortable, or else they have no traction in redirecting our lives. We "make time," or "go out of our way," or "reprioritize energy" in order explore the mystery of incarnation and come closer to Christ. The discomfort sharpens our sensitivity. It keeps us from surrendering to temptations that might sidetrack our attention.

  Take the medieval "hair shirt" as an example. There weren't many technologies back then to separate great lords from peasants, or the wealthy from the poor. Comfortable, fashionable clothing was one. Every serf sunburned by the land, or workaday knight with skin chafed by armor, longed for clean linen and smooth silk. To go the other direction and adopt clothing that was even rougher and more uncomfortable, or to turn one's jacket inside out so the smooth lining was outside and the rough fur against the skin ... now *that* was counter-cultural. It was a constant reminder. It kept one remarkably focused.

The mentor asks the seeker: *What is your hair shirt?* What will you introduce into your life that will be a constant reminder to focus on God, and a chronic discomfort that will counter the expectations of the world? Note that hair shirt strategies guard against hidden arrogance. No observer could tell if you wore a hair shirt. The prickling fur was *inside*.

- On the other hand, lifestyle ought to shape spiritual practices. If spiritual practices are too disruptive to your daily routine, or too foreign to your peculiar personality, you will fail to do them. You won't "enjoy" them. At best, you will feel chronically guilty. Spiritual habits should enliven, refresh, and empower you.

Take the artistic practices of plainsong, sculpture, stained glass, manuscript illumination, and painting for example. There weren't many opportunities for self-expression in medieval times, but these were especially incorporated into spiritual habits in endless variety and uniqueness. They encouraged individualization in an era of extraordinary uniformity.

The mentor asks the seeker: *What is your variation of the song?* How will you customize a spiritual discipline to express your personality? How will you adapt it to your work schedule? How will you fit it into your family life?

The challenge for the seeker is to find the right proportion of discomfort and comfort, the right mix of sacrifice and fulfillment, or the unique combination of "hair shirt" and "song" that enlivens and encourages the spiritual life.

For example, one seeker may have a middle management lifestyle that is remarkably sedentary, working nine to five on weekdays, spending weekends with the family, and having extra time for hobbies. The daily spiritual routine includes prayer with his or her spouse every evening, Bible reading over the noon lunch hour with printed commentary, and breakfast conversation at the diner every day. The weekly routine involves worship in one church 52 weeks out of the year, a face-to-face AA group every Wednesday night, and Friday evenings spent downtown in the homeless shelter. This person keeps a written journal by the bedside, never leaves the house without a hat with a phoenix symbol, and meets with the associate pastor every Saturday. The "hair shirt" is the homeless mission, and the "song" is the family.

Or, for example, another seeker may have a business lifestyle that is constantly mobile, unpredictable, and extremely pressured, working seven days a week and 24 hours a day. The daily spiritual routine consists of early-morning prayer, downloading scripture to a mobile phone, and intentional conversation with cab drivers, waiters, and sales representatives. The weekly routine involves worship in a different church and a different city every week, participation in a small group by way of text message and skype, and dedicating vacation time to social work. Ongoing accountability is dictated to a journal and sent to a confidential Google group, and this person recites the complete rosary whenever the plane takes off or lands. The "hair shirt" is the journaling and the "song" is the website.

Yet there is a challenge that emerges for both of these people, and for anyone customizing how they actually walk in companionship with Christ. It is the challenge of authenticity. Seekers do not want to play a part. They want to avoid pretence at all costs, and consider hypocrisy the worst of sins. They do not want to *pose* as spiritual people; they want *to be* spiritual people. To do that, they must know themselves.

There are already many resources to help us discern unique personality types and discover unique spiritual gifts. Personality typologies are all based on current psychological research, and are especially useful for appointing committees. Spiritual gifts inventories are all based on the experience of the earliest church, and are especially useful for designing entrepreneurial teams. Paul associates gifts with leadership roles in 1 Corinthians 12 and Ephesians 4, but clearly implies that spiritual gifts represent "abilities," "inclinations," or "passions" that are given to Christians to build the faith community and accomplish God's mission. It is entirely possible … and even divinely intended … that Christians should fulfill themselves *and* contribute to mission at the same time.

Mentors can help seekers discover and explore their unique personalities and spiritual gifts. Use whatever resource seems most useful for the particular individual. This is the easy part.

The challenge of mentoring in this stage is to guide seekers *to express* their unique personalities and spiritual gifts *consistently, openly,* and at times *courageously.* It is one thing to discover yourself, but quite another thing to be yourself. Personality inventories and gifts surveys are often merely interesting, but not actually life shaping. Participants require additional counseling and ongoing accountability. Two factors shape that counseling.

First, personality type and spiritual giftedness are both fluid rather than static. Personalities do evolve through life struggles and spiritual victories. Spiritual gifts are both discovered and revealed. Being oneself is a work in progress, and one that is not completely under one's control. The mentoring relationship is a means to discern these changes or to adapt to new circumstances.

The popular test for authenticity is to "feel good." If a particular pattern of behavior makes you feel happy, comfortable, or content, and if a particular set of activities brings you joy, satisfaction, or fulfillment, then surely you must be expressing your true personality and giftedness. That *may be* the case, but the mentor knows that it *may well not be* the case. Nothing is more comfortable and satisfying than returning to old ways, and those "good feelings" may actually disguise inauthentic living.

The real test for authenticity is that patterns of behavior and sets of activities *feel right.* They are appropriate to the experience of Christ and they are enhanced by spiritual habits. You may in fact feel temporarily unhappy, uncomfortable, or discontented, because you long for the personality that you are outgrowing, and the giftedness that was once so familiar. If "feeling good" causes seekers to distance themselves from the experience of Christ, or relax or abandon spiritual habits, then mentoring brings them back to what "feels right."

Second, at a more fundamental level, the self you once knew is being transformed into a "new creation" in Christ. Seekers justifiably want to be "true to themselves," but the "selves" to which they are "true" are being transformed by their relationships with Christ. "So if anyone is in Christ, there is a new creation: everything old has passed away; see, everything has become new!" (2 Cor. 5:17). The mentoring relationship is a means to understand and apply these changes to daily living.

The popular assumption is that there is an "authentic self" hidden within you. It may have been buried, ignored, or rejected for a variety of psychological or sociological reasons, but it remains to be discovered. It is a kind of primitive nobility, spark of genius, fundamentally sound integrity that simply needs to be turned loose on the world. There is certainly good within everyone, but the mentor knows that this inner self is far from perfect, and is often immature. Nothing has been so destructive in the world as arrogant self-actualization, and that "authentic me" may simply disguise an overweening ego.

In the mentoring relationship, the language of addiction is the best translation of the doctrine of original sin. At the heart of every person lurk self-destructive behavior patterns that we chronically deny.

> For I know that nothing good dwells within me, that is, in my flesh. I can will what is right, but I cannot do it. For I do not do the good I want, but the evil I do not want is what I do. Now if I do what I do not want, it is no longer I that do it, but sin that dwells within me. So I find it to be a law that when I want to do what is good, evil lies close at hand. For I delight in the law of God in my inmost self, but I see in my members another law at war with the law of my mind, making me captive to the law of sin that dwells in my members. Wretched man that I am! Who will rescue me from this body of death? (Rom. 7:18-24)

The point is that even the hidden, authentic self is incomplete. Grace transforms the individual into someone new.

The discernment and application of personality type and spiritual giftedness in real life is considerably more complex than inventories and surveys may suggest. Seekers who have come this far in the mentoring relationship may become frustrated.

○ *If all it took to feel good about myself was completing an inventory and survey, why did I bother to struggle with the experience of Christ and work so hard to build spiritual habits?*

○ *Why is it suddenly insufficient to just feel good about myself?*

The mentor replies that the theoretical insight into personality type and spiritual giftedness is not the same as applying it to daily living. Who you are now, and who you are yet to become, are different things. The goal of mentoring ... and the key to abundant life ... is not feeling good about oneself. Authenticity ultimately lies with aligning oneself with the purposes of God.

Mentoring builds incrementally on the discernment of personality and giftedness through three basic questions. Each question connects with a scripture for meditation. Authenticity becomes richer and deeper.

1) Who am I?

This is the benchmark established by personality and spiritual gifts inventories. It reveals what is "normal" for the unique individual, in the specific psychological and sociological context in which he or she lives now. Seekers reorient their lives to express their current identities. They change careers, reshape intimate relationships, and reprioritize time. Discovering the best about oneself brings satisfaction, but spotlighting the best also reveals the worst in shadowy relief. We are many personalities.

The story of Jesus' encounter with Legion (Mark 5:1-19) is a good place to begin this stage of mentoring. This is one of the few stories in which Jesus explicitly asks someone for his name. Identity lost and regained is the theme of the story. Legion, like many people today, has lost his identity to a host of "demons" that have frightened away the neighborhood (and presumably family, friends, and work associates). The name reveals his predicament, but it implies that his predicament is common to many. Legion is a kind of "Everyman" — his identity lost in the midst of multiple personalities. Yet even when he is restored to his right mind and exercises his will to follow Christ, God's higher expectation takes over. Legion's identity is to be found in his mission, of which he is told: "Go home to your friends, and tell them how much the Lord has done for you."

2) Who do I want to become?

The question is often prompted by an altered lifestyle. The changes a person makes in career, intimacy, and priorities may be natural, but surprisingly unsatisfying. Seekers want to be different people, not just do different things. People can change their personalities with practice and reinforcement, and they can choose to exercise and strengthen unused gifts. It is a matter of will power. The exercise of will, however, reveals unexpected powerlessness.

The Parable of the Prodigals (Luke 15:11-32) is also about finding oneself. There are two crises of identity in the story. First, the younger son follows his passion, squanders his life, and in the depth of poverty he "comes to himself" and remembers his father's benevolence (verse 17). He returns repentant and is given a hero's welcome. Second, the older son follows his duty, labors unceasingly, and in the depth of affluence resents his brother's welcome. The father remonstrates with him. Surely he knows that his inheritance is assured, and can spare some compassion for his long-lost brother! Modern seekers are not sure with whom they most identify. Who is *really* lost? And who is *really* found? Which lifestyle was really authentic? Which brother was deceiving himself the most? And does success have anything at all to do with authenticity?

3) Who does God want me to be?

This is often an "Aha!" moment for many seekers, as they finally begin to break beyond modern assumptions. The person God wants me to be may not be the person I really am, and may not even comfortably match with who I want to become. On the other hand, surrendering to God's re-creation will perfect who I am, and satisfy me in ways I cannot even imagine now. The advice from the first letter of Peter projects the vision:

Like obedient children, do not be conformed to the desires that you formerly had in ignorance. Instead, as he who called you is holy, be holy yourselves in all your conduct; for it is written, "You shall be holy, for I am holy" […] You have been born anew, not of perishable but of imperishable seed, through the living and enduring word of God […] Rid yourselves, therefore, of all malice, and all guile, insincerity, envy, and all slander. Like newborn infants, long for the pure, spiritual milk, so that by it you may grow into salvation […] Come to him, a living stone, though rejected by mortals yet chosen and precious in God's sight, and like living stones, let yourselves be built into a spiritual house, to be a holy priesthood, to offer spiritual sacrifices acceptable to God through Jesus Christ. (1 Pet. 1:14 and 2:5)

Personality and giftedness are not carved in stone. They are carved in *living* stone. Authenticity is more fluid and profound than we expected. The mentoring relationship guides seekers to see themselves in new perspective.

Snapshot

I came to know "Chris" as a teenager who was regarded, by peers and adults alike, as being "older than his years." Our paths converged for only two years when I was a youth pastor and he was an Eagle Scout. At the time I had no systematic understanding of mentoring, but it didn't take a genius to figure out that Chris was searching for his authentic self. These two years between High School and University would be critical.

This young adult was in obvious stress. He was living up to a lifestyle expectation imposed by his church, his father, and the exaggerated stereotype of leadership more suited to Teddy Roosevelt than to Jesus Christ. It was, after all, a conservative, affluent, New England community, and we were worshipping with a congregation that dated its history to before the Revolutionary War. Chris enjoyed considerable prestige, and was given unusual authority and responsibility. The more he chafed and fretted and rebelled against these constraints, the more he feared losing the respect he had gained. Once we established trust and confidentiality, he said to me that he felt more like an advertisement than a real person.

In those days personality inventories were new and imperfect, and processes to discern spiritual gifts weren't mentioned in the seminary curriculum. We did what we could. Our youth group was already highly committed to Bible study and dialogue, and we spent a great deal of time talking about diversity and uniqueness, mutual respect and reinforcement, alignment with Christ, and acceptance. Chris became more confident, less fearful of failure, and more aware of the many nuances and layers of his personality.

Most importantly, Chris became less judgmental and condescending. He actually recognized himself as the "older brother" in the Parable of the Prodigals. Respected, but lonely among his peers, he suddenly found himself basking in the fellowship of friends. About this time, he established his first really meaningful relationship with a young woman. His unrealistic dreams about his future began to give way to practical decisions about university majors and alternative careers.

This certainly satisfied church and community goals for youth ministry. Here was a young man who understood Christian faith, accepted social responsibility, and had some personal direction. Yet it wasn't enough, and he knew it. Our conversations continued as he sought to discern what God wanted him to be.

The reader will recall my anecdote of personal transformation describing the road trip with a youth choir and the counseling challenge after these young people performed in a state mental institution. The same incident was transformative for Christ (see pages 29-30). The "Aha!" moment for Chris came as a crisis. Remember that the youth choir was entirely unprepared for the experience of the hospital. It was so upsetting to these rather sheltered teens that emotions erupted as the bus trundled into the night after the concert. I don't know how many hours I spent kneeling on the cold, vibrating floor of the school bus, going seat to seat, comforting, encouraging, praying, and helping 13 - 18 year olds cope with their first experience of unexplainable tragedy. Only later did I learn that Chris had been on his knees behind me, picking up where I left off, repeating assurances, quoting scriptures, praying, and shedding tears of understanding.

After that, Chris had a gravity and purposefulness about his life and leadership that he had never had before. I think he had discovered what it meant to be God's servant.

Step 4:
Challenge the seeker to confront manipulation and temptation

The "good that I want to do, I cannot do; and the evil I do not want to do, I end up doing. Wretched man that I am! Who shall save me from this body of death?" (Rom. 7:19-20) The words of St. Paul continue to haunt us in the mentoring relationship. Spiritual growth is so *frustrating*. Seekers and mentors alike feel it. We deepen our experience of Christ, develop spiritual habits, and discover or shape our unique spiritual gifts and personalities. Yet again and again we feel distant from Christ, lose the discipline of spiritual habits, and ignore our gifts or contradict our own identities. Frustration is a chronic reminder of our imperfection.

Temptation is more complex and subtle than most people realize. It is easy to blame outside forces for sabotaging our spiritual growth. Controlling and manipulative persons are to blame, and we do assertiveness training to stand up to them. Perhaps it is a cruel boss, manipulative spouse, or the proverbial "mother-in-law." Perhaps it is the person who tempts us with alcohol, coffee, or cocaine, knowing that we are trying desperately to break the habit. Or perhaps it is the allure of promotion and power, sex and power, money and power, or anything at all *and power* that sidetracks us from spiritual maturity.

Historically, Christians have personified temptation as the devil. In addition to assertiveness training, Christians resorted to extraordinary tactics of "spiritual warfare" that were always external tactics ranging from prayers of supplication to exorcism. From the point of view of Christian mentoring, it is all ineffective because it fails to discern the complexity and subtlety of temptation. The tempter cannot "push our buttons" unless there are already buttons to push in our psyche. We are tempted to do only what our secret desire has pre-programmed us to do. We are manipulated only because, deep inside, we secretly want to be manipulated. Temptation is fundamentally an *internal* struggle making us vulnerable to an *external* force.

Mentoring relationships with Christians *who are part of the institutional church* are particularly susceptible to temptation. Most people associate "faith" with "religion" in its various trappings of institutional life, but unfortunately "religion" as an instrument of power and persuasion is consistently compromised by temptation, and often reduced to manipulation. What frustrates your pursuit of the spiritual life? Perhaps it is that peculiarly conniving and needy parishioner who always takes a jab at the pastor, or that peculiarly conniving and smooth talking pastor who always makes you feel guilty just when you are starting to feel good, or perhaps it is the multitude of meetings, the adulation of parishioners, or the lure of the large church.

"Control intervention" has long been a part of church transformation and church growth strategies. Leaders are encouraged to assertively confront "bullies" who seek to shape the church around their personal tastes, opinions, or lifestyles. Especially in small churches, it sometimes requires the loss of one or two selfish and domineering members in order to include many more seekers in a truly accepting environment. Yet there is a limit to "control intervention," just as there is a limit to assertive leadership. At what point do assertive leaders become controllers themselves? Where exactly is the boundary between preaching the Gospel and manipulating the agenda? What happens when the tempted become the tempters?

The earliest apostles, who were the first Christian mentors, had a much more profound understanding of temptation. They understood that temptation is a kind of vicious cycle of defeat, as internal weakness invites external manipulation, and external manipulation plays upon internal desires. There is a hidden controller in everyone, and the cycle of control and being controlled cannot be broken simply through assertiveness training and conflict resolution.

Blessed is anyone who endures temptation. Such a one has stood the test and will receive the crown of life that the Lord has promised to those who love him. No one, when tempted, should say, "I am being tempted by God"; for God cannot be tempted by evil and he himself tempts no one. But one is tempted by one's own desire, being lured and enticed by it; then, when that desire has conceived, it gives birth to sin, and that sin, when it is fully grown, gives birth to death. (James 1:12-15)

Paul worries that violent oppression may have preyed upon the weaknesses of Christians in Thessalonica and writes:

For this reason, when I could bear it no longer, I sent to find out about your faith; I was afraid that somehow the tempter had tempted you and that our labor had been in vain. But Timothy has just now come to us from you, and has brought us the good news of your faith and love ... Now may our God and Father himself and our Lord Jesus direct our way to you. And may the Lord make you increase and abound in love for one another and for all, just as we abound in love for you. And may he so strengthen your hearts in holiness that you may be blameless before our God and Father at the coming of our Lord Jesus with all his saints. (1 Thess. 3:5-13)

Jesus promises the apostles that he will send the Holy Spirit as an "advocate." The "advocate" breaks the vicious cycle of temptation.

And I will ask the Father, and he will give you another Advocate to be with you forever. This is the Spirit of truth, whom the world cannot receive, because it neither sees him nor knows him. You know him; because he abides with you, and he will be in you ... I have said these things to you while I am still with you. But the Advocate, the Holy Spirit, whom the Father will send in my name, will teach you everything, and remind you of all that I have said to you. (John 14:16-26)

The experience of the Holy Spirit is specifically aimed at breaking the vicious cycles of temptation that undermine faith and sidetrack the spiritual life.

Exactly how does the Holy Spirit intervene to break the cycle of temptation? Mentors guide seekers in seven ways.

> **The Vicious Cycle of Anger**

The cycle of anger is usually the first bitter fruit of frustration. Most Christians within the institutional church vent their anger initially on the *inertia* or *complacency* of the congregation or denomination. More profoundly, they may vent their anger at the mentor for encouraging self-discipline that is so counter-cultural. Or they may vent their anger at God for unexplainable evil. The more complacent that others seem to be in the face of unexplainable evil, the angrier the seeker becomes. But the angrier the seeker becomes, the more defensive churches are, and the more potent evil seems.

Mentoring breaks the power of this vicious cycle through *perspective* and *forgiveness*. Help the seeker understand the social and psychological reasons for such limited vision, and how unexplainable evil is paralleled by unexplainable grace. Awaken in the seeker a sense of pity and compassion, so that he or she might take the greater leap of faith, and forgive. Forgiveness is an act of the Holy Spirit. It does not erase the passion for justice, but it does eliminate the desire for vengeance. Forgiveness breaks the vicious cycle of manipulation and the resentment that it provokes.

> **The Vicious Cycle of Alienation**

The cycle of alienation often follows the cycle of anger. Metaphorically speaking, the "Tempter" is not done with you yet! Christians within the institutional church move to the margins of organized Christianity. They become cynical. Perhaps the parishioner now worships irregularly, refuses to serve in committees, and is publicly skeptical about God's mission to redeem the world. Perhaps the pastor worships mechanically, isolates him or herself from denominational or mission partners, and is publicly depressed about the future of the church. It is the *inflexibility* and *bureaucracy* of the church, governments, and educational institutions in general that is so annoying! The more inflexible that institutions are, the more alienated seekers become. And the more cynical and isolated the seekers become, the more the leadership vacuum among institutions is filled by reactionary people.

Mentoring breaks the power of this vicious cycle through *roots* and *relationships*. Help the seeker explore the origins of the Christian movement, his or her own denominational beginnings, and the ways in which bureaucracy is a mechanism for coping with fear. Connect the seeker with people who are making a difference to grow God's mission and change the world. Help the seeker to build cross-sector, cross-cultural, and international networks with people who have invested themselves in good work. Right relationships are creations of the Holy Spirit. Instead of a chorus of lamentation, participate in a choir of hope.

> ## The Vicious Cycle of Obsession

The cycle of obsession often follows the cycle of alienation. The "Tempter" is not done with you yet! Obsession is revealed by an inability to discern degrees of seriousness. Everything becomes a matter of life and death. The smallest details must be perfect. Every strategy must be immediate. It is the *dithering* and *obfuscation* of the church, and all institutions, that drive the seeker mad. The more the seeker observes people diverted by competing priorities, the more the seeker insists there is only one priority. All else (family, friends, job, health, and intimate relationships) are not only *less* important but *not* important at all.

Mentoring breaks the power of this vicious cycle through *humor* and *mission service*. Humor is a great leveler. It may even be sarcastic and mocking. Humor challenges seekers to observe their own foibles and laugh at themselves. It reveals the ironies and paradoxes of daily living. Mentors guide seekers to shut down their minds and work with their hands. Resign from the board and do hands-on service. Instead of perfecting the strategic plan, go with the flow. Learn how to opportunistically resolve unexpected problems. Live with the ambiguities of managing time and energy. The Holy Spirit pokes fun at the essential inadequacy of human thoughts and actions.

> ## The Vicious Cycle of Doubt

The cycle of doubt is often a reaction once the cycle of obsession is broken. Seekers laugh at themselves and immerse themselves in the ambiguities of service, but go too far. The "Tempter" uses even this to undermine spiritual growth. The more seekers are surrounded by *dabblers* and *doubters*, the more they are tempted to think irony is all there is. Hearty laughter turns to bitter jeering. Absolutes become mere perspectives. God's purpose is lost amid natural selection. Faith is a matter of opinion; morality a matter of taste. The more dilettantes just dabble in religion, and the more that the world reverts back to old habits, the more that seekers doubt the promises of God. And the more they doubt, the more the world dabbles.

Mentoring breaks the power of this vicious cycle through *persistence* and *persuasion*. Encourage the seeker to endure setbacks and keep going. Recover the original experience of Christ, build on the paradox of incarnation, and explain the reasonable consistency behind doctrines of sin and grace, free will and providence, and fallen existence and the hope of reconciliation. The Holy Spirit gives reassurance through purposeful living, and uses reason to convince people yet again of the truths of the Gospel.

➢ **The Vicious Cycle of Guilt**

The cycle of guilt often accompanies or follows the cycle of doubt. It is provoked by *accusations, complaints,* and *grudges* expressed by people within or beyond the church. The "Tempter" uses the criticisms of others to sting the faithful and undermine their confidence. No matter how diligent they are, seekers are led to believe it is not enough. No matter how caring they have tried to be, they are blamed for neglect. No matter how virtuous they try to behave, they are accused of hypocrisy. Knowledge of their own imperfections lends credence to such abuse. Seekers feel ashamed of their own hidden doubts, and count themselves unworthy of the mentor's attention and confidence. The more grudges, the more guilt, and the more guilt, the more vulnerable we become to smaller and smaller grudges.

Mentoring breaks the cycle of guilt through *acceptance* and *penance.* Perhaps acceptance includes forgiveness, but often guilt thrives on faults that barely deserve to be "forgiven." It is the accumulation of petty mistakes that generates the most despair, which is why the mean-hearted always catalogue the foibles of the clergy. Mentors *accept* seekers as they are, blemishes included, and in doing so assure them of the acceptance of God. The final goal, *self-acceptance,* is often the hardest to achieve. The Holy Spirit uses *penance* as a method of modest pain and practical obedience that helps seekers accept themselves. The only way to escape the legacy of "doing things wrong" is to "do something right."

> ## The Vicious Cycle of Arrogance

The vicious cycle of arrogance is often an extreme reaction to doubt and guilt. The "Tempter" uses our very success against us. Arrogance is an exaggerated confidence in one's own superiority. It is a claim to perfection, or at least to being among the best, most pious, most obedient servants of God. Arrogance may be provoked by the praise of others, public adulation, and lavished honors. It is sometimes *deliberately* provoked to set up the seeker for a fall. Arrogance permits one the discretion to relax behavioral standards and spiritual disciplines. The more adulation, the more arrogance, and the more arrogance, then the more that adulation is deliberately encouraged.

Mentoring breaks the cycle of arrogance through *role reversal* and *menial service*. These are the practical applications of an attitude of humility. Role reversal means that the seeker steps away from official, prestigious, public positions, to deliberately work at something entirely different — something that lacks power, prestige, or notoriety. This may especially involve menial labor. The seeker steps away from the podium to scrub floors. He or she does chores that are intentionally designed to deflate the ego, and that allow one to become sensitive to the life struggles of ordinary people.

> ## The Vicious Cycle of Accommodation

Whenever arrogance remains unchecked, the cycle of accommodation is inevitable. Accommodation relaxes standards of behavior and spiritual expectations in order to achieve harmony with the congregation or the world. In a sense, this is the last "temptation" because it leads to a complete contradiction of the spiritual life. The "Tempter" encourages people as they respond to arrogance by dividing into the two camps of "fans" and "critics." Each camp exaggerates its perspective, forcing leaders to compromise themselves by adapting to public opinion. Accommodation accedes to the comfort zones of the people. But the more their comfort is honored above all else, the harder it is to achieve, and new accommodations become required.

Mentoring breaks the cycle of accommodation through *courage* and *vision*. Once humility is rediscovered, the seeker turns back to God, rather than to public opinion, as the source of approval, and as a reference point for purpose. The seeker once again has the courage to confront the comfort zones of culture, dare to endure criticism, and cast a bolder vision of God's future for the church or the world.

These seven cycles of temptation may occur at any time, in any order, and are never completely overcome. At any point they may threaten to break the mentoring relationship because intervention by the mentor is often unwelcome by the seeker. Each of these cycles is, paradoxically, self-satisfying. It seems odd to say that a vicious cycle of anger, alienation, obsession, doubt, guilt, arrogance, or accommodation might actually be "comfortable" for the seeker, but that is often just the case. There is a perverse self-satisfaction in living an angry life or an alienated life. People live in false nobility when they are obsessed. They feel oddly "normal" living in doubt or guilt, because that seems to be the state of everyone else. They have a false sense of security in arrogance. Accommodation allows them to be just "one of the guys" and "everyone's friend." When the mentor seeks to break any of these vicious cycles, he or she is liable to be attacked and rejected.

My commentary may have conveyed hints of application specifically to clergy. The church (and institutional religion in general) is often an arena of intensified temptations. Clergy and lay leaders are often caught in any one of these vicious cycles of temptation as the behavior of the congregation and clergy becomes trapped in mutual provocation.

- The more inert the church, the more angry the clergy become. And the angrier the clergy become, the more entrenched and resistant to change the congregation becomes.

- The more inflexible church bureaucracy is, the more alienated the clergy become. And the more maverick the clergy become, the more inflexible and bureaucratic the church becomes.

- The more church members do ministries badly, the more obsessed the clergy become to do all ministries. And the more the clergy micro-manage, the more the laity protect their turf.

- The more the church dithers, the more the clergy doubt. And the more doubtful they become about God's purpose, the more the church looks for proofs and certainties.

- The more church people blame the clergy for failure or incompetence, the more the clergy feel guilty. And the more guilty the clergy feel, the more vulnerable they are to criticism.

- The more church people praise the clergy for success or achievement, the more the clergy exaggerate their importance. And the more arrogant the clergy become, the more likely people are to rebel.

- The more church people rebel, the more the clergy accommodate. And the harder the clergy try to preserve harmony, the more they are required to compromise.

The institutional church is often an experience of rarified temptation, much the way bacteria cultivates in a petrie dish. This is because it is an "official" religion, and regarded by the state as an agent of socialization. Any institution that has been given great responsibility will become a hotbed of control, and will be targeted with great temptation.

The wisdom of the first mentors, the apostles, ensured that regular worship would enhance the mentoring relationship. Worship can reinforce the interventions of mentoring that break the vicious cycles of anger, alienation, obsession, doubt, guilt, arrogance, or accommodation. The liturgical rite of *confession* encourages church leaders and members to acknowledge their comfortableness with temptation. The assurance of pardon encourages church leaders and members to *reform* their daily habits and mission priorities. Finally, the benediction and commissioning that concludes worship focuses church leaders and members on the bigger *vision* of reconciliation and redemption that God has in store for the fallen world.

Yet Christian seekers who stand apart from the institutional church are at risk as well. The same seven vicious cycles can beset their family lives, intimate relationships, and work environments. Mentors help them to see how they become trapped by temptation. The "Tempter" uses behavior and circumstance to "press the buttons" of vulnerability within each person, and uses the weaknesses of each person to shape relationships and situations around self-interest rather than divine purpose. There are risks whether you are a part *of* a Christian community, or apart *from* a Christian community, as the original solitary hermits and yoked monastic brothers discovered. The experience of history, however, indicates that in the end the communal life is more helpful to spiritual growth than the solitary life.

Snapshot

Christendom is disintegrating all around us, although at different speeds in different contexts. The pilgrim's progress of many clergy has been stopped at this stage. "John" was typical. He grew up Christian, entered seminary directly from university, followed the denomination routine for ordination, served three churches for about five years each, and moved up the career ladder from associate to senior pastor, and from rural to small city church. Reaching his 50's, John discovered that nothing was stable, reliable, or predictable anymore. Church members were hyper-critical. Judicatories were divided and dysfunctional. The public was indifferent or hostile. His marriage was rocky, and his family was frazzled. He had a chronic ulcer. And to top it all off, John was wondering why the "joy of the Lord" wasn't such a strength anymore.

I was able to walk with John for several years as I coached pastors in the regional judicatory. John has been through all seven vicious cycles of temptation ... some of them several times ... and is probably not out of the woods yet. Yet he has been making progress.

John's frustration first expressed itself as anger. His sermons became increasingly fiery, and he was increasingly animated in committee meetings. He lost a sense of perspective. He became remarkably timid about major issues of injustice and unbelief, and raged over seemingly small acts of unkindness and selfishness. This was because he understood that the spontaneous deeds of daily life reveal the real purity or corruption of an individual, and he saw the increasing faithlessness of church members, and the shallowness of culture. I helped him understand the broader, more radical shift to post-modernity, and we worked harder to restore personal spiritual disciplines. For John, the vicious cycle of anger and the vicious cycle of guilt were closely connected. He was angry at himself. He thought it was his fault. But once he had perspective, he found forgiveness.

Alienation followed the anger and guilt. John withdrew from the denomination, and disconnected with his clergy peers. He was frequently critical of the inflexibility and bureaucracy of churches, and the irrelevance and pedantry of seminaries. He heartily distrusted the smiles and handshakes of clergy, for he knew they covered up backbiting and competition that had reached Machiavellian proportions. We worked together to help him build fresh relationships, across public sectors, with leaders who were compatible with his personal values and purposes. I led him to rediscover his roots in the ancient church, and specifically in the cultural turmoil of the earliest mission to the gentiles.

Obsession and doubt are cycles of temptation that were, and still are, threatening to undermine John's spiritual life. John has become a perfectionist, particularly about liturgy, preaching, and administration. He takes himself, and his priestly tasks, seriously on an unhealthy level. Even his wife thinks he is pompous. She has stopped attending church out of her own anger, but privately confides that it is also because she can't stand her husband in the pulpit. "He is a different person than the loving man I know at home." Making fun of him has a spiritual point, and usually he can look in the mirror and laugh at himself. Yet this must be accompanied by mission service. I enlisted the help of his wife to push him to become more personally active in outreach with people beyond the church. It is here that he becomes most human and most Christian at the same time.

Ironically, doubt is the flip side of obsession. The more John obsessed over liturgy, the more he doubted the truth of the message within the liturgy. The more he practiced great oratory, the more he questioned the Gospel. The better he administered the church institution, the more he lost sight of the bigger vision. Aesthetics and politics became more important than theology and pastoral ministry. Slowly and persistently we returned our conversation to the paradox of incarnation, and the mystical experience of Christ, that was the source of his original calling to ministry as a young man.

Once John got over his anger, forgave himself for past mistakes, shaped a new and trusting peer group, checked his obsessive behavior, and recovered the experience of Christ, his church actually began to grow again. Indeed, his was the only church in the entire judicatory that was growing significantly. Not all were refugees from other churches. Many were seekers looking for big visions, credible leaders, and a chance to change the world. Now, however, John experienced the vicious cycles of arrogance and accommodation.

First, John got arrogant. He still is. If he doesn't change, it will kill him and his church. He has only begun to wrestle with it. Although he is self-deprecating in his speech, and lavish in his praise of others, John *really enjoys* being a success. He's written a book. He's lecturing in his denomination about church growth. He dresses casually, but has an uncanny ability to seek the limelight. He denies that his role is very important ... but as he ponders retirement he can find no plan for leadership succession. When he goes, the church will decline. And what does that really reveal about his leadership? So we have been trying to persuade John to turn over both responsibility *and authority* for leadership. He has been experimenting with role reversals. He is even doing small and (from his exalted perspective as change agent) menial chores. Today he is contemplating abdicating from leadership in his large church, and starting a new church plant in another city.

Second, John is accommodating to culture. He denies it, of course. He still preaches and teaches a counter-cultural message. Yet he drives a sports car, enjoys a larger salary than any of his peers, vacations at his own cottage, and golfs with his cross-sector peer group with remarkably little conversation about mission. He is growing conservative. He talks about risk, but doesn't take any risks. His church is doing extraordinary outreach locally and regionally, but that has more to do with abundant and well-managed resources than with love and compassion. The equity of the church is not really at stake.

Slowly, John is becoming uncomfortably aware of this. He is even aware that it is the Holy Spirit that is making him uncomfortable with the trappings of success. He is going on monastic retreats. He is fasting. He is gathering the courage to surrender to another of God's visions.

Step 5:
Connect the Seeker with the Accountability
of a Faith Community

Seekers may be members of an institutional church or alienated from the institutional church. In the post-Christendom environment today, many of the most earnest seekers are now at the margins or even outside the church. Throughout the mentoring process, it is helpful for seeker and mentor to be a part of a "faith community" because it helps them explore the experience of Christ, persist in spiritual habits, and clarify spiritual gifts. It is often only at the point of *frustration* and *temptation*, however, that seekers fully appreciate the value of the faith community.

This can be a difficult connection to make. Institutional churches can sometimes be the worst environments for manipulation and temptation. Seekers need a faith community to help them break the vicious cycles of anger, alienation, obsession, doubt, guilt, arrogance, or accommodation ... just as addicts need a support group to break the power of addiction. Yet many institutional churches actually mirror and model these same vicious cycles of anger, alienation, obsession, doubt, guilt, arrogance, and accommodation. Not just any faith community will do. Mentors connect seekers specifically with churches that help them overcome powers of manipulation and temptation.

If we examine the varieties of church life from the perspective of mentoring, we can see that there are five characteristics of churches. Size and denomination are not relevant here. Every healthy church combines all five of these characteristics, but one of these characteristics will dominate the others. This means that the system of accountability will shape itself around that dominant characteristic:

- **Praying:** Church worship may be very formal or informal, but corporate and personal prayer will be extremely important. The order of worship on Sunday morning will be very important, and faith will be a matter of understanding and agreeing with doctrines of the creed. Accountability will focus on Sunday morning worship attendance, participation in the sacraments, and correct understanding of the catechism or creed.

- **Caring:** Congregational life will be primarily about mutual support and personal counseling through the cycles of life, from birth to death. The fellowship of Sunday morning will be very important, but faith will be a very private matter for individual members. Accountability will focus on observing core values for harmony and respect, and taking responsibility for visitation and compassionate outreach.

- **Serving:** Membership expectations will emphasize financial support and community service. Church participants will be actively serving the governance structure, supporting denominational activities, and implementing social service and evangelism projects. Accountability will focus on sacrificial giving of time, talent, and money; and maintaining standards for excellence for all programs within and beyond the church.

- **Balancing:** Congregational life will emphasize healthy lifestyles, and programs will help people balance the many demands of marriage, family, work, and service. People will find help to cope with stress, keep perspective, and simplify and prioritize daily living. Accountability will focus on maintaining holistic health patterns, success in business, stability in relationships, and inner peace.

- **Discipling:** Congregational life will be designed to perpetuate a continuous cycle of life change, spiritual growth, discernment of call, continuing education, and personal mission. People will be expected to be passionate, make extraordinary sacrifices, and reshape their lifestyles around Christ. Accountability will focus on small group participation and mentoring relationships.

A faith community in which *discipling* is the dominant characteristic is the most helpful for the mentoring process. The *praying* church can help seekers clarify their experiences of Christ. The *caring* church can help them develop spiritual habits. The *serving* church can help seekers discern personality and spiritual gifts. None of these churches, however, are very effective in breaking the vicious cycles of anger, alienation, obsession, doubt, guilt, arrogance, or accommodation. They struggle to help seekers overcome manipulation and temptation.

Churches that are primarily about "balancing" lives and lifestyles are particularly unhelpful for seekers in mentoring relationships. This is because mentoring does the exact opposite. The outcome of mentoring is not a "balanced" life but an "unbalanced" life. It is a life of passion, rigorous alignment to mission, and extraordinary self-sacrifice. Seekers in a mentoring relationship tend to be viewed as "fanatics" in churches where *balancing* is the dominant characteristic. Unfortunately, *balancing* is the dominant characteristic of many large, contemporary churches.

I emphasize that all five characteristics are found in healthy churches, but the system of accountability in any church is shaped around one dominating characteristic. Mentors can see this in the way churches resolve conflicts, clarify policy, prioritize budgets, initiate programs, and even develop property. *Discipling* churches are often newly planted churches, house churches, and churches that are maverick to their denominational parents. They are churches that are visibly focused on experiencing Christ. They assertively train and model spiritual habits, encourage small group partnerships, deploy leaders by calling rather than by recruitment, and evaluate success. These are the churches with which mentors connect seekers. The mentoring relationship is integral to the expectation of these churches, and not a happy coincidence.

The basic unit of accountability, however, is not the church as a whole. It is the cell, team, small group, or (as I call it) the "pilgrim band" that may exist within any given church. It is possible for a church shaped around any dominant characteristic to still provide a great environment for mentoring ... *provided they nurture the Pilgrim Band.*[10] Every small group has an affinity. The affinity of this group, however, is to achieve the perfect alignment of one's personal life with God's purpose.

The idea of pilgrimage as spiritual discipline is common to many world religions. It began in Christianity in the 4th century, immediately after Constantine legitimized the church. The mother of the emperor initiated several pilgrimages to visit sites associated with Jesus, and she was soon imitated by scholars, ecclesiastics, and ordinary peasants. Their inspiration came from Scripture. Jesus intentionally returned to Jerusalem for the Passover in the company of his disciples. During the journey, he used the surrounding countryside, observations of people, and historic sites as teaching tools to mentor the faithful.

Pilgrim companionship became more important from medieval times onward as an additional protection for travelers. Despite the popularity of pilgrimage as a spiritual discipline, it is estimated that over half the pilgrims who set out never returned. Many were victims of brigands, disease, accidents, and border wars, which led to the establishment of "hospitals" and "hostels" by monastic communities along the way. The very dangers and temptations of the *physical* journey intentionally mirrored the dangers and temptations of the *inner* journey of spiritual growth.

Eventually the *inner* journey became the focus, and Christians practiced spiritual disciplines in the companionship of a small group wherever they were. The journey became objectified in liturgy through the stages of the cross, walking a "labyrinth," and other means. Dante's long allegory of redemption is framed as a pilgrimage with mentors (Virgil and Beatrice) who guide him through hell and purgatory to paradise.[11] Today the best way to understand the power of pilgrimage as a spiritual discipline is to read accounts of the Muslim "Hajj" (pilgrimage to Mecca). There you can recapture the spirit of mutual support, courage in the face of danger, desire for perfection, and anticipation of grace that were once typical of Christian pilgrimage.

---

[10] I first described the "Pilgrim Band" in my book *Talisman: Global Positioning for the Soul* (St. Louis: Chalice Press, 2006).
[11] Perhaps the most readable translation of Dante Alleghieri's *The Divine Comedy* was prepared by Allen Mandelbaum (New York: Alfred A. Knopf, Everyman's Library, 1995).

It may be easiest to recreate the experience of the pilgrim band in a church dominated by the characteristic of discipling, but it is possible to create such a group within any church, and even beyond the church. The pilgrim band is the primary "faith community" of mentors and seekers within the larger institutional church. Every pilgrim band has three characteristics.

First, the pilgrim band takes seriously the spiritual identity of the congregation. This identity is shaped by the consensus of people around core values, bedrock beliefs, motivating visions, and strategic mission. I have defined these in several places, and described how consensus is built.[12] Many church consultants describe this functionally as the foundation of trust that preserves integrity and encourages creativity. However, this consensus of identity in the institutional church is often considered an ideal rarely achieved by members, and preached (but not thoroughly practiced) by the staff.

Pilgrim bands take this consensus seriously. They strive to model the core values, or positive behavioral expectations, of early Christian people, which were originally set out by the earliest church (see Galatians 5 and Romans 12). They stake their lives and livelihoods on bedrock faith convictions to which they turn for strength in times of trouble or stress, and explore these in scripture, historic creeds, and the examples of saintly leaders. They shape their lifestyles around the vision and mission of the church, often making significant sacrifices in family stability and career advancement. In other words, pilgrim bands take the core values, beliefs, vision and mission of the church seriously. They routinely hold one another accountable for their failures, and advise one another in self-improvement. Therefore, they are often perceived as "elders" or "spiritual leaders" of the church — at least in credibility, if not in official leadership.

Second, the pilgrim band is a close companionship of mutual support. Spiritual growth must break the vicious cycles of manipulation and temptation. All members of the pilgrim band know that they cannot break the cycles of anger, alienation, obsession, doubt, guilt, arrogance, and accommodation alone. They must rely on each other for forgiveness, friendship, perspective, faith, forgiveness, humility, and courage. When they stumble, others can catch them before they fall. When they are

---

[12] For further information on this topic, refer to my books *Moving Off the Map* (Nashville: Abingdon Press, 2004) and *Spirited Leadership* (St. Louis: Chalice Press, 2008).

assaulted, others can come to their aid. When they are tempted, others can intervene to show them the right way.

It is really this kind of intimacy for which most seekers long, but two things block their path. On the one hand, institutional churches often provide only mere friendship, or limit personal support to periodic crisis intervention. On the other hand, western culture has privatized religion, creating the illusion that individuals can break the cycles of anger, alienation, obsession, doubt, guilt, arrogance, and accommodation on their own. The experience of the pilgrim band emerges only in times of an institutional emergency or a community crisis, but tends to disappear again when normality returns.

Third, the pilgrim band journeys to a holy destination. This clear spiritual destination was objectified in ancient times as Jerusalem (or other shrines and places that were stepping stones, as it were, to get to Jerusalem). Yet it is clear from even the most ancient accounts that the objective destination was only a sign of an *inner* destination. The goal of the pilgrim band is to be fully with God ... to experience unity with the divine ... to lose oneself in the greater mystery of Christ. This is the "New Jerusalem" that merges heaven and earth, where God is fully with the people, and tears shall be no more (Rev. 21).

There is something apocalyptic about the expectation of a pilgrim band. It is the destination, not just the journey, which is important. Together, they are going somewhere in particular, and not just exploring ideas. The holy destination, like the New Jerusalem, is both outward and inward. The outward destination is justice for all. The inward destination is unity with Christ. Their journey is a "crusade" in the original, spiritual meaning of that word. They anticipate the expectation of the Lord's Prayer: "Thy Kingdom come, thy will be done."

Theologians would argue that these three characteristics should be true for the church itself in any institutional form. Seekers will tell you that institutionalized Christian churches of all kinds have strayed far from this, and if on rare occasions they came close it didn't last long. The pilgrim band has a better chance to succeed. It is not only smaller, but it is unencumbered by property, polity, and salaried personnel. It is highly mobile, communicates over long distances, readily adapts to new circumstances, and is remarkably resilient against intimidation. The hope of the institution is that this is where your leaders come from. They do not come from nomination processes and denominational appointments. They come from the brotherhood or sisterhood of the pilgrim band.

The mentoring relationship eventually cries out for the accountability of the pilgrim band. Mentors may be able to connect seekers with an existing group within a local church ... especially if that local church is dominated by the characteristic of discipling. It may be a mega-church or a micro-church, a newly planted church or a house church, a cell structured church or a missionary church. It must be a church with an embedded foundation of trust, and a clear consensus for values, beliefs, vision, and mission. It must also be a church that is unafraid to host radical Christians in its midst, and therefore a church that is willing to take risks and stake harmony for the greater purpose of establishing God's reign on earth.

Therein lies the difficulty. Western churches in particular have become too clubbish and timid to welcome a pilgrim band into their midst. Mentors are looking elsewhere to connect seekers with pilgrim bands. Faith-based non-profit agencies, and even faith-based for-profit companies, are springing up everywhere. They invest enormous amounts of time and energy to develop leaders, involve employees in the corporate mission, and combine profits with positive social change. Pilgrim bands are emerging in every sector of culture, including sports and entertainment, government service, and the military, as seekers try to fill the vacuum of meaning left behind by modernity with a sense of personal destiny.

The three characteristics of the pilgrim band (spiritual identity, mutual support, and holy destination) point toward the practical accountability of the mentoring relationship. We need to set aside modern prejudices and fears about accountability based on task management and political correctness. This kind of accountability is designed to benefit the task masters rather than the workers. Mentors speak of accountability in the original meaning of the ancients. This kind of accountability is intended to benefit the workers themselves. It holds them accountable for their own maturity and for the fulfillment of their own lives.

Over the centuries, many have tried to define the "vows" that are required in order to participate in the pilgrim band. Much of the terminology, however, is nuanced in ways that are foreign to contemporary life. Mentors prepare seekers to commit to the following simple rules of the pilgrim band:

- **Tough Love**

Each member of the pilgrim band is radically honest with the others, and expects radical honesty in return. There may be affirmation or criticism. The affirmation may be surprising and occasionally embarrassing, carrying with it a heightened sense of responsibility. The criticism may be unexpected and hurtful, carrying with it a demand for repentance and change. All of it is guided, however, by the unwavering desire to bless the other and to help the other grow.

Tough love is as difficult to administer as it is to receive. Since members of the pilgrim band really do care for one another, they may be hesitant to speak the truth, waiting for a "right time" that never comes. We may be fearful of hidden manipulations in ourselves, using affirmation or criticism as a means of advancing our own authority. The more honest we are, the more we risk honest responses. Even if we risk anger, or endanger the relationship itself, it is all for the purpose of the mutual growth of the brothers and sisters of the pilgrim band.

- **Steady Concentration**

Members of the pilgrim band prioritize time and energy to think for themselves. They do not simply mouth slogans and creeds, or waste time in idle chatter. They ponder the relevance of the core values and beliefs that they hold precious to the business of daily living. They consider the sources of faith through scripture, biography, and prayer. It is a *steady* concentration that permeates lifestyle, and is not limited to an hour of study or a burst of attention.

Steady concentration is perhaps more difficult today than ever before, given the distractions of the highly mobile and multi-media world. Helping one another multi-task and still focus is part of the mutual accountability of the group. Group members share insights with one another, ask questions, and engage dialogue, and when the thread wanders each member refines the point. Steady concentration is really not about reading and meditation, but about lively conversation and shared insight.

■   **Expanding Compassion**

Each member of the pilgrim band connects the internal dialogue of the group with external interaction with culture. The pilgrim band is not a fan club for specific kinds of tastes and opinions; it is not a society for the preservation of any particular culture. It is just the opposite. It is eclectic. It is attentive to the diversity of cultures and the diversity of needs surrounding them. A true pilgrim band is always learning a new language, appreciating a new cultural form, and exploring individuality more than collectivity.

If one person becomes more sensitive to the needs and life struggles of people around them, how much more sensitive will the combined observation of the group be? Each member calls the attention of the others to the experiences of life going on around them. Individually and as a group they reach out to bless others in practical ways, encourage others by sharing the insights of a pondered faith, and pray for others as they follow their own paths.

It should be clear that the pilgrim band is different from traditional church fellowship groups because it draws participants into a much deeper intimacy. Accountability is not focused on amiable relationships, but on encouraging one another for spiritual growth. It is also different from traditional church small affinity groups because it reinforces a disciplined spiritual life. Accountability is not focused on learning facts or enjoying common interests, but on breaking the vicious cycles that block spiritual growth.

Imagine, then, what a contemporary pilgrim band might look like. The small group of spiritual travelers may include men and women, young and old, and people of diverse cultures and interests. Each person takes seriously the spiritual identity of core values and beliefs, and each commits to the spiritual growth of the others. Members meet weekly over breakfast, trade emails that affirm and critique, communicate insights and raise questions, and alert participants to the emerging needs of others. Even as they are physically far apart, traveling to different countries, they continue to be in conversation (through facebook, twitter, and whatever new method of instant dialogue emerges next month).

They constantly pause in their journey together to help others. They do whatever they can to heal the broken, befriend the lonely, guide the lost, bring justice to victims, give hope to the anxious, and offer the entrapped a fresh start. Every act of compassion is inspiration for the deeper reflection that they share with one another. If one member of the group is caught in a cycle of anger, alienation, obsession, doubt, guilt, arrogance, or accommodation, the others rescue him or her through tough love. If one member is in need, anywhere in the world, the others fly to his or her aid. All of this is done as part of a *journey*. After all, they are pilgrims traveling to a holy destination. Nothing stops or sidetracks them for long. Their ultimate goal is the New Jerusalem ... justice on earth and unity with God in Christ.

Mentors connect seekers to the accountability of such a faith community. This is more than a referral to join a church. It is engagement with a pilgrim band. If they can find this faith community within the institutional church, that's wonderful. If they can find this faith community beyond the institutional church, that's fine too. Mentors may or may not be a part of each pilgrim band, but do have a role in shaping seekers' capacity for fellowship, and for teaching them the "rules" of tough love, steady concentration, and expanding compassion.

Most importantly, the mentor keeps seekers moving toward the holy destination. Like all pilgrim bands, there is always a temptation to stop, settle down, enjoy the fruits of their labors, and linger with a limited number of people. To be blunt, there is always the temptation to buy property, build a structure, organize a board, hire a pastor to our liking, lock in a liturgy, develop an operating budget ... and plant a church! Pilgrim bands are not really church planters. At least, they do not plant anything remotely like an institutional church. They must keep on the move, and the role of the mentor is to keep them restless for God.

Snapshot

Individualism is a dominant characteristic of modern western culture, and even the social networking and peer groups of post-modernity have done little to counteract this predisposition. We have all encountered people who believe they can live a Christian life on their own, and think they do not need to belong to a faith community. I have mentored seekers through all the previous stages of spiritual growth, and even helped them see the necessity of peer group support in enabling them to resist vicious cycles of temptation. Nevertheless, their spiritual lives plateaued when it came to accepting the accountability of a faith community.

"Laura" is a case in point. Our conversation really began when she and her fiancé sought a church with a center aisle where they could have a wedding. Our church insisted that the center aisle and marriage counseling came as a package deal, so we began a conversation. She and her fiancé fit the stereotype of church drop-outs very well. Laura had been converted at 13 in a church camp, attended Sunday school until confirmation, experimented with life and spirituality in university, and returned to faith in Christ through a campus fellowship. She actually did have spiritual habits for Bible reading and prayer (although they were *very* flexible and suffered gaps of neglect). She was quite confident in herself and her goals. She had been alienated from the church, and angry at religion for some time, although now she was blandly tolerant and a little amused by churchy people in general.

She understood the importance of Christ, tried to live a worthy life, and saw no point in the overhead expectations of the church. She said (and I believed her) that she could pray, care, and serve on her own ... and that cooperating with the politics, pettiness, and rigidity of churchy people actually got in her way. She was well on her way to leading a balanced life through self-help books and yoga. The call to disciple new Christians would best be fulfilled by raising a Christian family. Why church?

My response was to focus on the key word "accountability." We skipped the usual marriage counseling agenda. We didn't bother to talk about communication skills, conflict resolution, sexuality, or parenting responsibilities, and the details about the wedding were settled in 15 minutes. Instead, I pressed the question: Why Church? That led us to re-examine her assumptions about her conversion to faith, her later reaffirmation of faith, and her real sincerity and purpose behind Bible reading and prayer. We focused especially on how she handled the vicious cycles of manipulation and temptation. This last made her fiancé nervous, and it was at this point that he finally joined the conversation.

Part of the mentoring focused on tough love. I aggressively challenged the couple to reveal the hidden faults, failings, mistakes, injustices, and downright evils of their limited life experiences, and sought to unveil the self-delusions, co-dependencies, and coercive relationships that shaped their lives ... and that they chronically denied. There were some heated moments! However, we shaped these bits of conversation around an intentional covenant of acceptance and forgiveness, and always focused on the purpose of such self-examination to deepen trust and self-confidence. It became clearer and clearer to Laura that the shared tasks of her social service partners, and the easy friendship of her yoga class, were not really sufficient to help her in her struggle with the vicious cycles of temptation and manipulation in life.

Part of the mentoring concentrated on faith. I ignored any review of dogma and doctrine. Instead, I challenged her to declare what was "bedrock" in her belief. We explored incidents when she was pushed to the limit of endurance ... talking about her potentially terminal illness, recent car accident, death of beloved parents, and so on. In each case we explored those absolute convictions to which she turned for strength in times of trouble. We discovered that she had less faith than she thought she had, and less courage than she probably needed to have.

Finally, part of the mentoring expanded her sense of compassion. Was raising a Christian family enough? Jesus himself rarely alluded to it, and never really talked about it. Slowly her heart began to enlarge, and began to burst for others who were strangers to grace. Since Laura and her partner were getting married, this led to a frank discussion of all the weird relatives and "skeletons" in the closet of each family. We also explored local and global needs. They personally experienced selected mission projects among people who were outside their normal circle of relationships.

Our conversation continued after they were married. They returned about a year later to talk about baptism for an expected child. In the intervening time, they had actually done little to build on the spiritual journey we had begun. Laura was in much the same place as before ... except that her anxiety about child bearing, and child rearing, was pushing her to think again about Christian accountability. We renewed the covenant of honesty and forgiveness. Tough love, concentrated faith, and expanding compassion returned as themes.

Eventually the baby was baptized in congregational worship and, according to doctrine and the polity of our denomination, became a "member of the faith community." Laura, her husband, and I were under no illusions, however. Laura's alienation and hidden anger about the church had not gone away, and she had the maturity and awareness to own it. They never even promised to come to Christmas Eve services because she understood the hidden hypocrisy of a church connection based on sentimentality. I never even asked them to join the church.

I did encourage them to join a small group. There were a number of independent house churches, Bible study groups, and other intentional Christian communities emerging in their nearby area. All of them took accountability for Christian life and mission far more seriously, and personally, than the established churches of the community. A couple of these small groups were sponsored by our church, or included a number of our young adults as singles or couples. I urged them to join one of these groups. Only through such a group would they ultimately return to Sunday worship. And one day, years later, accompanied by close companions from such a small group, there they were.

Step 6:
Encourage the seeker to discern
his or her personal mission in life

The mentoring relationship began with a quest to discern one's personal mission. "Quest" may be too strong a word, at least in the beginning. The seeker may simply express the desire for growth, maturity, personal fulfillment, satisfaction, clarity of purpose, or the general confidence that he or she is living life well. The seeker originally comes to the mentoring relationship out of restlessness, bearing many questions and frustrations, or because he or she is generally dissatisfied with the "way things are going." There has to be more.

There is a memorable quote from the Christian existentialist Soren Kierkegaard that has influenced many authors and spiritual guides. It influenced me long ago when, as a young man, I studied history and theology in St. Andrew's, Scotland during a year abroad from my college. Kierkegaard said "we all come to life with sealed orders."[13] At first we are unaware of them, but when the time is right an inner compulsion drives us to break the seal and discover what God has in store for us. We discover our purpose with the *fear and trembling* of a soldier about to be redeployed, or a pilgrim about to embark on a journey.

The difficulty with Kierkegaard's insight is that his language suggests that our mission purpose must be a particular career, job, or role. Yet modern and post-modern people know full well that the average person changes career paths five times in his or her life, works at a multitude of jobs (often overlapping one another), and plays many different roles in the world. Some roles fit and are comfortable to perform. Some roles do not fit, and feel awkward to perform. Some roles seem to come naturally, and in those roles people find success to be routine. Some roles seem fundamentally foreign, and in those roles people find failure to be common.

---

[13] Sören Kierkegaard, *Fear and Trembling*, Tr. Walter Lowrie (Princeton: University Press, 1970); John P. Schuster mentions the same passage in his book *Answering Your Call* (San Francisco: Berrett-Koehler, 2003), 18.

From the point of view of the soldier or pilgrim, "comfort," "success," "joy," and "satisfaction" may be clues to identify our callings, but they are unreliable. Soldiers or pilgrims may do things that are uncomfortable, distasteful, personally unsatisfying, and with a high potential for failure ... and yet they know in their hearts that *they must do it.*

Many mentors interpret Kierkegaard's concept of the "sealed orders" as a reference to the essence of an activity, rather than to an activity itself. It is a common denominator — a characteristic or quality that lies behind, or infuses any particular career, task, or job. So long as you are creating a thing of beauty, or inventing an opportunity to bless another human being, it doesn't matter if you are mopping floors or painting masterpieces. You have the heart of an artist and the spirit of a philanthropist. John P. Schuster writes:

> Calls command that you attach yourself to something infinite and lasting, so that you can escape the life you thought you deserved and replace it with the life you were meant for.[14]

It is easy to read that passage and assume that the "life you thought you deserved" was menial, painful, impoverished, or trivial, and that the "life you were meant for" must be powerful, happy, important, and full of wealth. That is not what Schuster means. This is why Kierkegaard and Christian spiritual guides throughout history admonish us to approach our "calls" with "fear and trembling." In the end, the clues to personal mission are more profound. Personal mission is less about passion, and more about noble sacrifice. It is less about success, and more about loyalty. It is less about power, and more about righteousness. It is less about happiness and more about a deeper, abiding serenity.

John Wesley is representative of a long line of historic Christian leaders whose restlessness drove them to open God's "sealed orders." Many biographies record similar quests that did not end in identifying *a job to be done*, but by describing *an attitude to live.* Wesley's powerful prayer from his famous "Watch Night Service" reveals the sense of personal mission for many historic Christian figures:

> I am no longer my own, but thine. Put me to what thou wilt; rank me with whom thou wilt; put me to doing, put me to

---

[14] John P. Schuster, *Answering Your Call* (San Francisco: Berrett-Koehler, 2003), 14.

suffering; let me be employed for thee or laid aside for thee, exalted for thee or brought low for thee; let me be full, let me be empty; let me have all things, let me have nothing; I freely and heartily yield all things to thy pleasure and disposal.[15]

There is still much for seekers to explore as they learn what they can do, at any given time, to contribute to a greater purpose. But it is important to set this exploration in the right context. What count in the end are not the tasks we perform, but our relationship with God. Augustine says it succinctly: "Our hearts find no peace [Lord] until they rest in you."[16]

I mentioned my first encounter with Kierkegaard and his comment that "we all come to life with sealed orders." My trip to study in the divinity school of St. Andrew's was the first trip in what has become a lifetime of journeys to different places, through which I have met different peoples, and experienced different cultures and careers. Although traveling to Scotland is hardly a perilous journey, it was a traumatic moment for a sheltered Midwestern boy like me. In those days the trip required several means of transportation, but through the entire journey the same refrain from a then new and popular song kept running through my head:

Dance, then, wherever you may be;
I am the Lord of the dance said He;
And I'll lead you all wherever you maybe;
I will lead you all in the dance said He.[17]

It was a particularly odd song for me to remember because I have a very poor sense of rhythm, and I am a remarkably ludicrous dancer. Nevertheless, the refrain haunted my days and nights. The abiding questions were: What exactly is the dance? Is it still going on even if I don't hear the music? And what new dance step do I have to learn next, despite my inadequacy?

The destiny of any Christian is to perfectly align him or herself with God's mission to redeem the world. So long as you are aligned to that purpose, any given activity, task, or career will either be shaped to fit, or will eventually be abandoned. Mentors help seekers place themselves in a

---

[15] John Wesley, "An Order of Worship for Such as Would Enter into or Renew Their Covenant with God," *The Book of Worship* (Nashville: United Methodist Publishing House, 1965), 387.

[16] Augustine, *Confessions* Tr. R.S. Pine-Coffin (Penguin: London, 1966), 21.

[17] A Shaker melody with words by Sydney Carter (Stainer and Bell, 1963).

continuum of infinite purpose, which is expressed through a series of relationships.

We all know that a line connects two points. Yet it is quite a leap to connect, on the one end, God's mission to redeem the world, and on the other end, my personal mission that participates in such a huge goal. Therefore, other points must be defined on the continuum. These other points are things that help us place ourselves ... or help us be placed by God ... in the larger scheme, which aims to reunite the infinite and the finite, creator and creation, heaven and earth. Of course, it is harder to draw a *straight* line through multiple points, especially in the chaos of change and perspective that marks our progress in life.

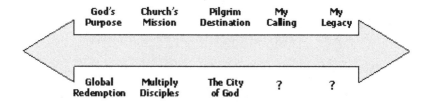

The broadest relationship in which we discern our personal missions is the relationship between God and the world. Whether or not we use metaphors of fallenness, the separation between life-as-it-is and life-as-it-should-be is obvious. Existence may reveal the good, the beautiful, and the true, but whenever goodness, beauty, and truth are seen they are undermined by evil, ugliness, and falsehood. Death, corruption, sorrow, and pain can only be partly explained by free will. Beyond human responsibility, and beyond human capacity for improvement, there is something fundamentally wrong with existence.

I am speaking, of course, to *Christian* mentoring. The reasons why people might believe in God, or recognize the infinite purpose, is not the point of mentoring. Once people do believe in God, or recognize infinite purpose, mentors help seekers come closer so that they see it more clearly and participate in it more fully. Mentoring without belief in God or infinite purpose is reduced to mere counseling for personal satisfaction, balanced living, and material success. But if one *does* believe in God or infinite purpose, one realizes that there must be something more to human destiny. Mentors help seekers grasp this "something more." If nothing else, mentors motivate seekers with a dream, a vision, and an expectation that *some day* and *somehow* the separation between existence and God will be eliminated.

Timeliness

However, mentors can do more than motivate. If timelessness is blocked by time passages so that nothing good, beautiful, or true endures for long, then *timeliness* is perhaps the most significant way in which people can unite themselves with God's purpose. *Timeliness* is a personal initiative that is *timed just right*. It is the perfect deed at just the right moment ... in the *"nick of time."* This is similar to the experience of *kairos*, which the ancients described as a breakthrough of the fullness of God in a moment of history. Yet in this case it is not God's intervention but *our* intervention that is so timely.

Mentors guide seekers to hone their gifts for *timely intervention.* Look back on your personal history. Describe the occasions when your words or actions were "just right." In each of those situations, just one action or word proved to be the decisive influence — the "tipping point" — that blessed another with healing, friendship, guidance, hope, self-esteem, or a fresh start. The more synchronized your chronological living is with the purpose of God for redemption, the more that these "timely" acts will occur.

We tend to dismiss the *timeliness* of our actions. "Isn't it lucky I happened to be there?" "I just had a feeling it would help!" Mentors help us to attune our intuition. As we become clearer about our own life struggles and experiences of grace, and about our own personalities and spiritual gifts ... and as we become more disciplined about our spiritual habits and more accountable for tough love, steady concentration, and expanding compassion ... our intuition becomes more finely honed. A spontaneous deed and an unrehearsed word were not just "lucky" coincidences, nor were they dependent on our mood at the moment. Instead, we had poised ourselves to seize the opportunity when it arose.

We also tend to exaggerate our responsibility for the *timeliness* of our actions. "I was just waiting for it to happen!" "Well after all, that's my job!" Mentors challenge us to be aware of our hidden desires to be in control, and of our tendency to manipulate events to appear "timely" when they are not. We remove our egos from the experience, and understand ourselves to be part of a flow of Spirit, but not in control of the Spirit.

Mentors guide seekers to explore the patterns of their *timeliness*. Do they find themselves to be especially good at certain kinds of beneficial interventions, or specifically attuned to certain kinds of needs? When they let themselves go, abandon themselves to the Spirit, and mentally step back to see what happens ... *then what happens?* What results? Does the *timeliness* of their deeds reveal a predisposition for healing, befriending, guiding, encouraging, building self-esteem, or opening new possibilities for others?

Holiness

The second relationship in which we discern our personal missions is the relationship between the church and the world. I do not speak now of any particular institutional church. I speak of the universal church, or the ideal faith community, and its primary purpose to go into all the world and make disciples of Jesus Christ. The connection between the "invisible" and "visible" church is a complex subject. What exactly are "disciples," and how does one align one's life purpose to help the church multiply them?

Our support for God's mission to redeem the world is what defines discipleship. When Jesus is asked about the essence of faithfulness, he responds with the Great Commandment, his own paraphrase of Deuteronomy 6:5: "You shall love the Lord your God with all your heart, and with all your soul, and with all your mind." Jesus immediately references Leviticus 19:18, and adds a second commandment: "love your neighbor as yourself" (Matt. 22:37-38). Although there is much more to be said ... and debated ... that is the essence of faithfulness.

The "disciple" is one who stands at the intersection of the infinite and the finite. In this sense, his model and companion is Jesus the Christ, who did that and does that more perfectly than any human can fully imitate. Disciples seek unity with the divine (loving God with all their hearts, souls, and minds), and disciples seek justice in the world (loving their neighbors as themselves).

The "Great Commission" that defines the church is to multiply *those disciples*. Multiply people who have the courage, humility, wisdom, and compassion to stand at that intersection of the infinite and the finite. A "disciple" is one who loves the Lord and loves the neighbor above all things, even at the risk of his or her own life, and who teaches others to do so as well. A "disciple" is not only *standing* at that holy intersection, but is also *walking* in companionship with Christ, who reveals in his life and teachings that that "intersection" is actually experienced in daily living and fallen existence.

The historic paradigm of the "disciple" is Simon Peter. The defining moment in his life occurs after the death of Jesus, when he returns to his old career as a fisherman (John 21). The story that follows is clearly a greater analogy about aligning one's personal mission with the mission of the universal church. Peter and his companions have been working at their old careers with little result (i.e. no fish). The incognito Christ appears on the beach and tells them to let their nets down one more time. They do as instructed, and the result is a miraculous catch. Peter recognizes the resurrected Lord, leaps from the boat, swims ashore, and falls at Jesus' feet. Jesus asks three times a question that is clearly symbolic of his invitation to every believer: *Simon, son of Jonas, do you love me more than these?* Do you love the Lord with all your heart, soul, mind, and might? Are you willing to love your neighbor as yourself? Will you stake everything, including your career and the things you love most, on your love of me? The story ends with a reality check, as Jesus foretells what will happen to Peter, and to any disciple who stands at the intersection of the infinite and the finite. Discipleship is counter-cultural. It is dangerous business.

Mentors help seekers sharpen their experiences of *holiness*. These experiences of awe combine ecstasy and reality, promise and danger. The alignment of personal mission and divine purpose requires seekers to explore the *timeliness* of their initiatives, and now the alignment of personal mission with the church's mission requires seekers to explore the *holiness* of their experiences. Mentors help seekers look back on their personal histories. Rediscover the moments of *holiness* when you felt yourself at the intersection of the infinite and the finite. The ordinary things around you were filled with extraordinary import. The little details expanded into enormous significance.

We tend to sentimentalize our experiences of *holiness*. Our recollections are of beautiful sunsets, starry skies, placid waters, and a first kiss. Mentors help us go beyond emotion to see how *holiness* prompts courageous action and places us at risk in the world. It is a fearful thing to stand in the presence of the Lord. There is profound scrutiny. Penetrating questions hang in the air. Do you love me more than these? Do you love me more than pretty sunsets? Do you love me enough to allow God to disturb your serenity?

We also tend to over-dramatize our experiences of *holiness*. Our expectations are to speak in tongues, observe fire and brimstone, be blinded by dazzling light on the highway, or hear voices coming from thin air. Mentors help us go beyond personal drama to see how *holiness* siphons away ego and dreams of glory, revealing the simple goodness and embracing love of God. Gentle commandments come to mind. Feed my sheep. Feed my lambs. Share the abundance of life with the least of Christ's brothers and sisters.

Mentors guide seekers to explore patterns in their experiences of *holiness*. Personal mission becomes clearer as seekers intentionally try to stand at the intersection of the infinite and the finite. When, and in what circumstances, have we experienced *holiness?* How can we deliberately create opportunities or environments where others can experience *holiness?* We align our personal missions with God's purpose as we discover how to bring others to a life dominated by the love of God and the love of neighbors.

Progress

The third relationship in which we discern our personal missions is our relationship with the pilgrim band. The pilgrim band is that small group or team of people who hold one another accountable for spiritual growth, and who, together, journey through life toward a holy destination. One's personal mission aligns with the team's mission. The metaphor for that holy destination is the "New Jerusalem" where tears shall be no more and God shall be fully with God's people (Rev. 21).

St. Augustine expanded our imaginations by reinterpreting the "New Jerusalem" to mean the "City of God." He wrote on the eve of the sack of Rome in 410, but also during the rise of the Christian city of Constantinople. It was with the emergence of a shared Christian faith, and sensitivity to the diversity of urban life, that the "holy destination" of pilgrimage was freshly explored. Augustine argued that there are two communities, or "cities," on earth, which are commingled in the reality of urban life but eventually separated by the judgment of God. There is the city of those faithful to God, and the city of those who would rival God.[18]

Augustine's books that are gathered under the title *City of God* have historically been treated as *socio-political* because they define the spiritual role of the state, or the temporal role of the church. But the real point of his work is to describe the flow of salvation history, and the part

---

[18] Roy W. Battenhouse, *A Companion to the Study of St. Augustine* (London: Oxford University Press, 1969), 51-53.

played in that grand scheme by ordinary Christians. Life is a journey that one takes with trusted companions, headed toward one destination and away from another. However ambiguous our loyalties and decisions might be on any given day, there is still the choice (for which the pilgrim band holds us accountable) to go *this direction* rather than *that direction*. Personal mission is not really about *creating* the Kingdom of God on earth, but about *abiding* in the Kingdom of God on earth. The question for every seeker is this: Will this step take me nearer to, or further away from the City of God?

The impetus that drives spiritual growth, according to Augustine, is not the attempt to escape the trials and tribulations of the world, but to find real perfection. It is not that the world is bad, but that the world is not good enough. Whatever happiness we experience is still imperfect. Spiritual growth is about striving for perfection. Augustine's prose was later set to music, and it is not hard to imagine the pilgrim band walking down the road, avoiding temptations on the one hand, and doing compassionate deeds on the other hand, while singing a song:

> *And now we watch and struggle,*
> *And now we live in hope;*
> *And Sion in her anguish*
> *With Babylon must cope.*

> *But he whom now we trust in*
> *Shall then be seen and known,*
> *And they that know and see him*
> *Shall have him for their own.* [19]

The holy destination helps define the individual's personal mission. The seeker is on a mission, motivated more by self-improvement or spiritual growth than by rejection of the world. While the love of God and the love of neighbors shape our actions, the trajectory of our living is toward a particular perfection.

Our history and intentionality about *timeliness* and *holiness* have aligned our personal missions with God's purpose. Now our history and intentionality about *progress* align our personal missions with God's purpose. Mentors help seekers focus on the destination, avoid sidetracks, and evaluate each step. Looking back on the progress of our lives, has each

---

[19] Excerpted from Bernard of Cluny's *De Contemptu Mundi*, trans. by J.M. Neale. Quoted in Roy W. Battenhouse's book *A Companion to the Study of St. Augustine* (London: Oxford University Press, 1969)]), 278.

step moved us forward or backward? Are our lifestyles more synchronized with the harmony of God, or less synchronized? Will this career move, or that friendship, or those purchases, or these activities, or any particular decision on our part *move us forward* so that we abide in the City of God?

So far the alignment of our personal missions or callings with God's purpose has been defined by our relationships to the incarnation, the universal church, and pilgrim bands. Mentors guide seekers to discover their personal histories and intentionalities for *timeliness, holiness,* and *progress.*

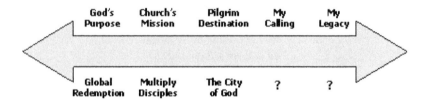

Now the mentoring relationship is more difficult. On any given day, the seeker asks: *What is my calling?* Clearly the calling is not any particular career, role, or activity. It is more about consistent intervention, abiding experience, and constant progress. Life may be an ever-changing mix of careers, tasks, relationships, and loyalties, but if our interventions to bless others, our experiences of the Holy, and our spiritual growth remains, deepens, and expands, then surely we must be on the right road to the City of God. But what is the right mix, right now?

Calling

The spiritual life culminates in clarity of purpose. All those steps in mentoring ultimately lead to the point where a seeker can finally know what God wants them to do. This is often described as a "calling", but if you have followed the mentoring steps this final discernment of purpose is actually a "re-calling". It is an opportunity to recall (bring back to conscious memory) what you are all about in the first place. What has been buried under distractions, manipulations, ambiguities, and deceptions is once again brought to light.

There are many clergy, for example, who become so immersed in the details of institutional life, cultural conflict, or pastoral routine that they lose their sense of original purpose. The passion and clarity of their original calling has been obscured. Clarity does not come from a weekend retreat, advanced degree program, or continuing education. It comes through the hard work of a mentoring relationship. Yet when all is said and done, they end up slightly amazed: *Now why didn't I see that before?* It is perhaps that obvious.

The call at any given point in your life is the intersection of three things: experience with Christ, awareness of personal potential, and insight into contextual opportunity.

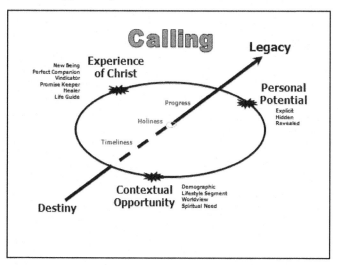

The steps of the mentoring process have focused this intersection of discernment.

First, the mentoring process has helped the seeker explore the different ways Christ is present in life, and the particular way Christ is relevant right now. They have identified the spiritual yearnings, in themselves and in the world, which motivates their search for God. They have customized and embraced spiritual disciplines that keep them connected with God as they experience the ups and downs of living.

Second, they have explored their authenticity as human beings. Some of their personality aspects, spiritual gifts, and skills have been explicit and are easily identified. Others have been unconscious or hidden, and are now intentional. Still others have been revealed: personality changes and spiritual gifts that are freshly bestowed by the Holy Spirit. The seeker has confronted the manipulations and temptations, in themselves and in the world, that sidetrack or block spiritual growth. They have new freedom and commitment to become what God intends them to be.

Now the seeker can look at the surrounding context in a new way. They can see opportunities for service. Notice how the mentoring process contrasts with typical strategic planning methods. Typically, people who are uncertain about the purpose of their lives *start* by identifying gaps and brainstorming innovations. Calling is confused with opportunism. "Opportunities" are nothing more than career moves. The mentoring process explores Christ experience and personal potential first, and *ends* with a systematic scan of contextual opportunities. A calling is not a career move. It is a "heart burst".

A "heart burst" is an awakened passion to bless a particular public. The life of St. Paul, for example, progressed one "heart burst" at a time. His strategic decisions were not guided by gaps and innovations that would advance his career, but by repeated "heart bursts" that involved considerable risk.

> "[Paul and his companions] went through the region of Phrygia and Galatia, having been forbidden by the Holy Spirit to speak the word in Asia. When they had come opposite Mysia, they attempted to go into Bithynia, but the Spirit of Jesus did not allow them; so, passing by Mysia, they went down to Troas. During the night Paul had a vision: there stood a man of Macedonia pleading with him and saying, "Come over to Macedonia and help us." (Acts 16:6-9)

The Macedonian in Paul's dream was a definable, describable public. These people lived a certain place, spoke a distinct language, ate different food groups, and probably listened to certain kinds of music. They also had specific physical and spiritual needs. Paul's heart broke when he saw the vision. Perhaps he wept. Certainly he felt extraordinary urgency to reach them. The call was probably not his *preference*. He would rather have gone to Bithynia. The call was probably not the best strategic plan. Greater opportunity for career success probably lay in Asia. Yet his heart burst for the Macedonian, and he risked everything to get to where the Macedonian lived.

Today we have very concrete tools to explore the diversity of the public.

- Demographic study investigates age, race, gender, income, family status, education, and occupation.

- Lifestyle segment study investigates daily behavioral patterns, social preferences, and common concerns.

- Psychographic study investigates attitudes, prejudices, worldviews, and moods.

The mentors can guide seekers to investigate the world around them in considerable detail thanks to the abundance of research tools today.

Yet that is not enough to discern call. Sensitivity to the experience of Christ, and awareness of human potential, combine to see the public with fresh eyes. We can go yet deeper to discern spiritual needs. At different times, in multiple ways, people are particularly broken, lost, lonely, anxious, victimized, or trapped. In the very first step in the mentoring process, we discovered how these deeper spiritual needs motivate people to seek the immanence of God. Now the heart of the seeker meets the spiritual need of the public. The result is a "heart burst".

The call becomes clear as three things converge: experience of Christ, awareness of personal potential, and contextual opportunity. The previous chart envisions this as a kind of circular movement. Draw a straight line through the center of that convergence. That is the line that connects your destiny and legacy to God's purpose to redeem the world. The call becomes clearer as you contemplate the timeliness of your life at this hour of human need; the holiness of your life as you follow Christ to bless others; and the progress of your life that has prepared you for this moment.

What is the legacy you hope to leave behind? If it were possible for you to look back on your life the day after you die, what would you want to see? What will you have passed on to your children, friends, and the urban diversity at large on this planet? How do you want to be remembered? What accomplishments, even if they go unrecognized by people still living, will nevertheless make you proud? What positive social and personal changes will you see in retrospect and earn God's praise for?

What moments or actions from your life will lead God to say: *Well done, good and faithful servant*?

There is an old exercise that I remember doing in my teens. Our youth group leader asked us to write our own epitaph ... the words to be written on our tombstones. The responses were too vague and idealistic. What we really must do is pre-construct our own biographies. Mentors guide seekers to be concrete about our reputations. It doesn't matter what kind of eulogy is printed in the newspaper. What kinds of spontaneous conversations should be overhead before and after our funeral services? Or will our lives be quickly forgotten and conversations turn to other things?

Of course, it is not mere notoriety that challenges seekers to define their trajectories in life. One might be vilified after death for living a life that was true to God's purpose. One might be forgotten for years, and then suddenly remembered as a model and teacher. And one might be utterly forgotten by human history, and yet be a first citizen in the City of God.

Reflecting on one's legacy introduces the true "end point" that connects a straight line to God's purpose. It is not what we do today, but what we leave behind, that truly aligns our personal missions with the redemption of the world.

What is my calling ... right now? John Schuster offers a simple grid based on intersecting poles for "Head" and "Heart," and "Internal" and "External." He is writing for a broad audience. I prefer a tool designed specifically for Christian mentoring. Instead of a "grid," I call it a "scope." It is the kind of telescopic sight found on a sophisticated bow for modern archery.

Imagine that circle that depicted the confluence of your experience of Christ, awareness of personal potential, and contextual opportunity. Turn that circle on end, and prop it up as if it were a target. Select an arrow from your quiver that represents the alignment of your life with God's purpose of redemption.

Imagine a modern competitive bow, with a telescopic scope set on top. Setting aside considerations for wind, humidity, or other external factors, a rifle should fire a bullet in an absolutely straight line. So long as the scope is correctly set, a marksman should hit the center of the target every time.

This is an analogy for how a seeker focuses his or her personal mission. The "bow" is the individual person, looking down the shaft of the arrow, as it were, from the legacy that he or she hopes to leave behind, and toward the goal of God's purpose to redeem the world. The "scope" is his or her own spiritual life, and in the "crosshairs" the seeker can see beyond institutional and personal relationships, to the real heart of the matter. The center of the target is God's purpose for redemption. Call it the city of God, or divine destination that your heart bursts to reach.

The "crosshairs" are formed by the intersection of vertical and horizontal lines. These are a means to evaluate the authenticity of a calling at any given time in your life.

- The vertical line is the continuum of "joy" and "urgency." Your personal calling at any given time is always a combination of those two things. The more your personal mission is a *joy*, the more you want to savor it, and the less urgency you feel to act. The more your personal mission is *urgent*, the more you are driven by compulsion or necessity, and the less pleasurable is the act. This vertical line adjusts to focus on God's mission for the redemption of the world.

- The horizontal line is the continuum of "unity" and "justice." Your personal calling at any given time is also a combination of these two things. The more your personal mission is about growing in *unity* with God, the more inward and passive you may be, and the less involved in human affairs you may be. The more your personal mission is about *justice*, the more outward and interactive you may be, and the less time you will spend on introspection. This horizontal line adjusts to focus on God's mission for the City of God.

Just as it is with a real telescopic scope, the smaller lines on the crosshairs help you make corrections for any external circumstances that bear directly on the discernment for personal mission. As you aim at the target of God's purpose, you adjust your aim up and down out of consideration for marriage, family, and interpersonal relationships. Similarly, you adjust your aim from side to side out of consideration for ethical ambiguities, political realities, or theological concerns.

However, just as the rifle and the scope are connected and yet distinct items, so also are the actual daily existence of the seeker and the seeker's ideal spiritual life connected and yet distinct from one another The smallest irregularity between the rifle and the scope will cause the bullet to miss the target ... sometimes by a wide margin. Therefore, there is an inevitable weakness in the connection between spiritual life, and life as it is actually lived. We might call this weakness sin. We simply recognize that, the human condition being what it is, "the good that I want to do, I fail to do; and the evil I want to avoid is what I end up doing." We may see very clearly how we want our legacy to align with God's purpose, but find that our goals and actions at any given time take us in altogether different directions.

Imagine, therefore, the Olympic target shooter posed to take his shot on this particular day, at this particular stage in his life. He is suddenly overwhelmed by doubt. Despite his best efforts, *is the rifle truly aligned with the scope? If he fires, will his shot be a hit or a miss?* The same quandary possesses the seeker deciding on his or her personal mission. The mentoring relationship has helped you do all that can be done to discipline your life and connect you with God's purpose. But when it comes to an actual decision between this career or that career, or between getting married or not getting married, or between this course of action or that course of action, you hesitate to pull the trigger. Doubts set in. *Is this really what God wants me to do? Will this really be timely, holy, and a positive step in the right direction? If I do this, will it be a hit or a miss?*

There is only one thing to do if you are an Olympic athlete. The coach tells the athlete to fire a test shot. Afterward, the athlete peers carefully through the scope using the crosshairs for accurate measurement, and sees if the bullet hit the center of the target or was off the mark. The coach guides the athlete to make adjustments.

Something similar occurs in the mentoring relationship. The mentor tells the seeker to "fire a test shot." Imagine as precisely as possible, with as much detail as possible, what will result from any important decision and action (career, marriage, joining a church, ordination, relocation, accumulation of wealth, distribution of wealth, going to war, going to peace, or any other significant action in the whole range of possibilities). Imagine yourself doing that. Then look through the "scope" of your emerging spiritual life and see if your action hit the target.

For example, Fred decides to enroll in a business college where he can use his gifts for accounting and management, idealistically believing he can make a difference in the world from within a corporate career. Several years after graduation, he is successful in business, enjoying a great income, and serving on the boards for several non-profit agencies. He is also unhappy and unfulfilled. Fred and his mentor peer through the "scope" of his spiritual life to discover that his initial education and career choice had missed the mark (See #1 on the chart above). Yes, he was doing something enjoyable and related to justice, but his action was too far removed from the central target of God's purpose.

So Fred decides to resign from the corporate office, take a less responsible job, spend more time with his family, attend church more regularly, and dedicate himself to earnest prayer (See #2 on the chart above). But even though Fred's balanced life of "family values," "simplicity," and "health and fitness" are celebrated in the surrounding culture, and even though he and his wife spend their vacations building orphanages in a foreign country, Fred comes back to the mentoring relationship frustrated and cynical. Once again, he and his mentor peer through the "scope" of his spiritual life, and Fred sees that he was missing the mark.

Next, Fred decides to get out of business entirely. He becomes the CEO of a faith-based non-profit organization. The foundation raises, manages, and invests millions of dollars in a variety of good causes. Although it is serious business, Fred is having the time of his life flying around the world, investigating social service initiatives, advocating human rights, and actually seeing measurable results. He is making a difference in making the City of God into a reality. He has now realized the value of a continuing mentoring relationship, so when he begins to feel guilty about his happy lifestyle and the tragic predicaments of his clients, he and his mentor look through the scope of his spiritual life (See #3 on the chart above). While it is true that he is finally coming close to the target, Fred realizes that his life is largely spent in just one quadrant.

Fred leaves his management position with the foundation, renegotiates his marriage relationship with his wife, and together they relocate to live in a poor community. They learn a second language, personally manage a local social service agency, and Fred uses his accounting and business savvy to help neighborhood people start their own businesses. His life is more troubled than before. He is anxious for his children at school, and his family occasionally has to go without some life necessities (and a lot of luxuries), but he has an inner compulsion to serve. Eventually, however, he finds himself physically and mentally exhausted. He is feeding others, but not really being fed himself. He and his mentor look yet again through the scope of his spiritual life (See #4 on the chart above), and see that he is still very externally focused, but has replaced joy with duty as his life motivation.

Now Fred works for an ecumenical church council in the urban core of the city. He is taking a few courses at a nearby seminary, and is very active helping plant a new church. He encourages his wife to pursue a separate career, and their marriage is more harmonious than ever. (She has her own mentoring relationship). People say that Fred is more spontaneous, serene, and funny than he ever was before. He wants to leave a legacy of being a friend to different cultures, a tutor for organizational leaders, and a guide to younger seekers. Looking through the "scope" of his spiritual life, he might not be hitting the absolute center of the target, and perhaps he never will, but he is closer than ever before.

Snapshot

Much of my work has been spent helping clergy "re-mission" themselves in the middle of their careers. The clergy drop-out rate from traditional parish ministry is startlingly high, but it is actually not often driven by anger at the church, and is almost never driven by doubts about faith. In my experience, most of the many clergy who are leaving parish ministry are driven out by boredom, and by a general lack of self-fulfillment. They often begin our conversation by sharing feelings of listlessness, restlessness, and chronic frustration about the pettiness and routine of ministry. They ask questions like: "Is that all there is?" They often make comments like: "I am eager to go deeper and further with Christ ... but no one else is."

"Alice" was a young minister in her second pastorate, and her first as sole pastor. She was passionate about church growth, and committed to transformational ministry in a small town in Louisiana that was being overtaken by urban sprawl. Hurricane Katrina interrupted the process, but Alice found a new direction of ministry, coordinating shelter for the homeless and rebuilding their homes. The presenting problem was that the long term impact of the hurricane had reduced Alice's congregation by about 50%, and almost eliminated the core of lay leadership. Conflict in the church around change and outreach made Alice more and more discouraged ... and she began questioning whether or not she was really going in the right direction.

We began to explore the origins of her calling, and her real hopes for having an enduring impact on God's realm. Her extraordinary compassion for the homeless refugees of the hurricane became more focused. Her greatest sense of urgency was for victims of abuse as well as circumstance, and she actually found more joy in life bringing people back from the brink of despair than preaching sermons and administrating a church. Alice chose to leave traditional parish ministry to train for chaplaincy.

Step 7:
Release the seeker to God's mercy

The final step in the mentoring relationship is to let the seeker go free, and to commend the seeker to the mercy of God. The mentoring relationship is often unpredictable. We move forward, then go back to revisit past steps, and sometimes there are gaps in the conversation. We try to organize the mentoring relationship into covenants that can be renewed and redesigned as we go along, and the overall relationship may last days, weeks, or years. Nevertheless, both the mentor and the seeker eventually sense that the time has come to stop. The mentor has given about as much as he or she can give, and the seeker has received about as much as he or she can receive.

A particular mentoring relationship, like any relationship, can eventually become more of a hindrance to spiritual growth than a help. It can become a comfortable habit, filled with a great deal of affection. But whenever the preservation or perpetuation of a relationship becomes *more important* than the spiritual growth emerging from it, the relationship needs to end. This does not mean that the *friendship* needs to end, but that the intentional practice of:

✓ Leading Questions,
✓ Challenging Assertions,
✓ Decisive Interventions, and
✓ Pregnant Silences,

is not longer effective. The friendship can remain, but the mentoring relationship must be established with someone else.

This decision to end the mentoring relationship is not easy to make. The seeker has been *positively* dependent on the guidance of the mentor, and the risk is that the seeker and mentor might become *co-dependent* in their relationship to one another. The seeker requires the affirmation of the mentor to continue in spiritual growth, and the mentor requires the affirmation of the seeker to continue to be confident in guiding spiritual growth. The minute that seeker and mentor become consistently comfortable with each other, they are no longer *staking* or *risking* themselves for spiritual growth. The true seeker is *always* anxious about staking his or her life on spiritual growth, and the true mentor is *always* anxious about staking his or her life on giving advice for spiritual growth. The moment the ambivalence of "Yes and No" leaves their relationship, effective mentoring ends. Mentors are always worried about their incompetence: "This may be right ... but it may be wrong." Seekers are always worried about their inexperience: "This may be constructive ... but it may be dangerous." When the mentoring relationship becomes so confident and comfortable that mentors are *certain* and seekers are *sure*, the risk goes out of the relationship and effective mentoring ends.

The first thing that blocks closure to the mentoring relationship is the "Seeker Complex." This refers to seekers who are convinced that they are "never quite ready" to take responsibility for their own spiritual growth. The seeker perpetuates the mentoring relationship out of fear, not expectation. The reality is that no one is ever ready to take responsibility for their spiritual life. The experience of Christ will always be a mystery, and never fully grasped. The mission of God will always be vast, and never fully completed on this side of existence. The vicious cycles will never be completely broken and rendered powerless. The journey to the New Jerusalem is a long one, with unexpected twists and turns. The point is that there will never be a time when we are absolutely competent.

The "Seeker Complex" means that the seeker clings to the mentor the way that a capsized sailor, in fear of drowning, clings to his rescuer. They must catch their breath, calm themselves down, focus on the distant shoreline, and eventually swim for themselves. If they don't, both will drown. There is no *guarantee* that the capsized sailor will reach the shore. Who knows? A shark may attack, a hidden reef may intervene, or a cramp may slow them down. But unless they have the courage to swim for themselves, the hope of salvation will vanish.

Seekers often begin a mentoring relationship with childish naiveté. They soon learn that the alignment of one's life with God's purpose is more difficult and demanding than expected. Yet even after they have considerably matured, the inner child re-emerges on the brink of independence to hold them back. Like teenagers leaving home for the first time, they look back with frightened eyes. The mentor must wave encouragement, but close the door.

The second thing that blocks closure to the mentoring relationship is the "Savior Complex." This refers to mentors who are obsessed with the idea that they are ultimately responsible for the salvation of the seeker. The mentor perpetuates the mentoring relationship out of ego-centrism, not mission-mindedness. The reality is that no one can take ultimate responsibility for anyone else's salvation. Some seekers hit the target, and align themselves with God's purpose with near perfection. Some will come close. Some will miss the target altogether. Some will do well for a time, and then fall prey to one of the vicious cycles of temptation. The point is that the mentor cannot control the futures of others.

The "Savior Complex" means that the mentor clings to the seeker the way that a rescuer clutches a drowning man, even after he is safe. The rescuer must hold tight, whisper encouragement, point out the distant shoreline ... and then give the other a shove in the right direction. Otherwise, the rescuer will become the drowning man. After all, mentors are not people that landed on the beach of salvation and then turned back to leap into the ocean. They are swimmers themselves. They were capsized. Someone else helped them to swim. They are swimming in the right direction. Along the way, they help others who are newly capsized. *But then they must continue swimming.* The journey of the mentor is not done either.

Mentors often begin a mentoring relationship with false confidence. They soon learn that helping others align their lives with God's purpose is more difficult and demanding than expected. Even as they accept the risks and ambiguities involved in helping guide others in God's purpose, their sense of guilt and potential condemnation increases. *What if* my guidance is poor? *What if* this seeker drowns anyway? *What if* my faith is misplaced, or my judgment is skewed, or my advice is poor? These mentors are like parents saying goodbye to their teenager for the first time. They are moved by the frightened eyes. But they must close the door, and pay attention to the next child.

The mentoring relationship, powerful and influential as it may be, is only part of a larger network of spiritual relationships. Some are visible. Other friends, colleagues, neighbors, church members, and strangers will take over responsibility for the next steps in spiritual growth and accountability. Since we often do not yet know who those people will be, we realize that the key spiritual relationship is invisible. Jesus promises to send the Holy Spirit as "counselor" and "guide":

> If in my name you ask me for anything, I will do it. If you love me, you will keep my commandments. And I will ask the Father, and he will give you another Advocate, to be with you forever. This is the Spirit of truth, whom the world cannot receive, because it neither sees him nor knows him.

You know him, because he abides with you, and he will be in you. (John 14:14-17)

Any single mentoring relationship is only a part of a series of mentoring relationships. Sometimes the mentor and seeker can see it, and the mentor literally hands off the seeker to another who can guide him or her in the next steps of the journey. Sometimes neither mentor nor seeker can see it, and both trust in the abiding presence of the Holy Spirit. The Holy Spirit does just what mentors do. The Spirit asks leading questions, poses challenging assertions, makes decisive interventions, and creates pregnant silences.

If we continue the metaphor of the capsized sailor who was first drowning, then rescued, and is now swimming on his or her own for the distant shore, mentor and seeker alike realize that the swimmer *appears* to be alone ... but *is not alone.*

If we continue the metaphor of the teenager leaving home for young adulthood, both mentor and seeker realize that the teenager *appears* to be alone ... but *is not alone.*

And if we use the language of dependency and co-dependency, mentors and seekers realize that all co-dependencies are idolatrous and destructive, because there is only *one* co-dependency that is divine and blessed. That is the co-dependency of the seeker with God. One way or another, the seeker needs God for the fulfillment of his or her life. And one way or another, God needs every seeker in order to complete the process of redemption.

The idea of bringing closure to a relationship by "commending the seeker to the mercy of God" sounds trite to modern ears. This is not just because Christendom has overused the phrase, and because its repetition in liturgy has made it sound pedantic and otherworldly. It is because there is a profound skepticism in modern times that God is, indeed, *merciful.* Many believe God exists. But most believe that God is, at best, *indifferent.* That God should actively ... or even habitually and strategically ... take an interest in *my* living is a surprise greeted by cynicism. Yet that is the foundation of all Christian mentoring.

If the mentor believed, deep inside, that God was indifferent to the seeker, or that he was haphazard about divine mercy, then mentoring would be unbearable. Who could live with the responsibility? Who could absolve themselves of guilt? And if the seeker believed, deep inside, that God was indifferent to his or her quest, or easily distracted by more important people and more desperate situations, so that chronologically speaking they were basically on their own, then mentoring would be a waste of time. Who could endure such self-discipline? Who could help you when you were helpless?

God's mercy is what comes before the mentoring relationship, and God's mercy is what follows the mentoring relationship. It is a small miracle that the mentoring relationship began at all, given the temptations of the world and the selfishness of human beings. It is another small miracle that spiritual growth continues after the mentoring relationship, given the very same conditions of existence. *Despite existence*, God's mercy endures. *Despite failures*, spiritual growth continues. *Despite the limitations of humankind*, there is a destiny for each individual human. The mentoring relationship is part of it all, but not the guarantee of it all. That lies with God.

Snapshot

Mentoring takes time, and one of the biggest obstacles to mentoring in the post-modern world is the incredible mobility of people. In many regions the average residency rate may be only 4-5 years, and in urban areas it may be measured in months. That's barely enough time to train church members to have skills, much less mentor Christians to discern personal mission. The mentoring opportunity may last years or minutes, and it may recur intermittently or return years after the original conversation.

Some time ago I phoned a company's toll-free number to order resources for my church. The woman on the other end of the line suddenly asked: "Are you the Tom Bandy who was a youth pastor in Chicago in 1973?" Cautiously answering in the affirmative, I learned that she had been connected with the youth group, and that what we had discussed during and after her brief period in jail had set her life on a whole new direction. Here she was, an unwed mother of two, gainfully employed, committed to Christ, and taking night school courses in social work. It turns out that there were other mentors in her life (including a pastor, a colleague, and a guidance counselor) who were all unknown to each other but collectively led her to discern her vocation.

More recently, I established a mentoring relationship with a small-town pastor who was trying to transform and grow a stodgy church with a history of conflict. He was a mature seminary student, opening a second career, having been called out of a lucrative job as a chemical engineer to serve the church. The denomination didn't approve of his innovative habits, so they advanced him beyond his capabilities to lead a difficult church, hoping that he would give up the ministry and go back where he came from. Many of his clergy colleagues were jealous of the appointment and minimally helpful.

He came to me initially for coaching. Together we helped him equip himself, develop a strategic plan, and actually grow the church. However, it soon became apparent that his biggest challenge was to discern more clearly the mission that God had in store for him. Over the next year and a half we covenanted to monthly internet conversations, and occasionally met face to face. We explored all of the steps discussed in this book.

- He discovered the real presence of Jesus Christ in ways that were not part of his original conversion, but were now a vital part of his personal and family hope.

- He became ever more rigorous about his spiritual habits for daily living, and began to model and teach his own lay leaders to do the same.

- He explored his personality and spiritual gifts, accepted himself at his worst and expressed himself at his best, and became increasingly confident as a leader.

- He struggled over and over again with the temptations and manipulations that threatened his personal and professional life. He experienced cycles of anger, alienation, and guilt. He worked through his perfectionism and his theological doubts. He even faced his arrogance, and his temptations to accommodate to culture.

- Finally, he wrestled with his accountability to the denomination, and the unreasonable demands and financial burdens of seminary residency requirements that would separate him from his family.

It was at this point, when he began to use the methodology to discern personal mission in life, that circumstances beyond our control ended our conversations. I was both anxious and frustrated ... until my own experience with Christ rescued me from the temptations of arrogance.

I am just a link in the chain of providential relationships, and so are you. I suspect that I will again be in conversation with this Christian leader, and I anticipate being surprised by his progress and intrigued by his new questions. But if I am wrong, and never hear from him again, then my spiritual habit to pray for fellow pilgrims will continue. God's mercy never fails. Other mentors will emerge in his life, whether or not he recognizes the relationships as "mentoring," and whether or not the "mentors" understand the roles that they are playing in his life.

Letting go is one of the greatest leaps of faith. If it were not for the truth of incarnation and the conviction that God is fully human and fully divine, one could hardly do it. But since the God above gods is in the here and now, we can end one conversation and begin another.

Second Thoughts

After all this, perhaps you are having second thoughts. The mentoring relationship is less than you dreamed about, but more than you bargained for. It doesn't guarantee inner peace and the answers to life's biggest questions, but it demands a great deal of personal commitment and hard work. The mentoring role itself is probably less powerful than you hoped, but more influential than you dared imagine. It doesn't gain much prestige or lead to big incomes, but it causes people to make sacrifices and take risks for which you will be held accountable by God.

For awhile you said to yourself, *I can do this!* Later your self-doubts increased and you thought: *I can't do this!* You long to be a part of such a conversation along the way, and as a seeker you long to be mentored. However, to be a facilitator and guide for the conversation along the way, you doubt that you have the maturity or ability to be a mentor.

The mentoring relationship began as a "simple" process of imparting wisdom to the less experienced. The more we investigate this relationship, the more we discover how different it is from the other relationships with which modern people are familiar.

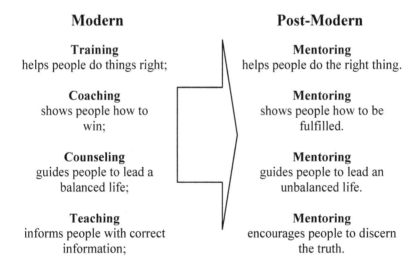

Modern	Post-Modern
Training helps people do things right;	**Mentoring** helps people do the right thing.
Coaching shows people how to win;	**Mentoring** shows people how to be fulfilled.
Counseling guides people to lead a balanced life;	**Mentoring** guides people to lead an unbalanced life.
Teaching informs people with correct information;	**Mentoring** encourages people to discern the truth.

The very assumption that mentors are always mentors, and that seekers are always seekers, has become increasingly complex. Mentors are just seekers who are further in the journey than the people they are mentoring. Seekers are just mentors waiting for an opportunity to guide those who come behind.

At what point does the seeker become a mentor? The answer is this: whenever someone with less experience is in need of help. It is the same thing with parenting. People do not become parents because they are ready to be parents. They become parents because, ready or not, they have a child on their hands.

At what point does the mentor become a seeker? The answer is this: whenever someone with more experience is ready to help. Again, it is the same thing with parenting. Adults do not ask questions of their own parents because they are incompetent. They ask questions of their parents because they are suddenly out of their depth.

Modern people are often alarmed when they find mentoring relationships to be so challenging. What did they expect? Is discerning your personal mission in life somehow easier than falling in love, getting married, and having a baby? Is companionship with Christ somehow less mysterious and eventful than growing up with a brother or sister? Is spiritual life somehow less stressful than building a career? Is spiritual growth somehow less strenuous than playing professional team sports? Is traveling to the New Jerusalem more carefree than following a roadmap to Los Angeles?

Many observers, from many fields, have observed the "reductionist" attitude that is implicit to modern living. Everything and anything can be miniaturized, simplified, and reduced to minimal components. The principle applies not just to technologies, but to vocations, relationships, and ideas.

- Vocation is reduced to career.
- Education is reduced to job training.
- Health is reduced to fitness.
- Love is reduced to sexual technique.
- Friendship is reduced to personality type.
- Success is reduced to power.
- Philanthropy is reduced to social service.
- Truth is reduced to information.
- Faith is reduced to church.
- Spiritual life is reduced to happiness.

Once the goals of living have been reduced, the processes to obtain these goals can be simplified, streamlined, and accomplished with relative ease (and modest financial investment). A curriculum, program, college degree, special training course, or self-help book will do. Or a therapeutic process, pharmaceutical prescription, or surgery will make it better. Modern people are more likely to seek a second opinion, but less likely to seek a mentor.

When modern people apply the same attitude of reduction to spirituality, separating out the "objective" value from the "subjective" dross, there isn't much left. The only marketable, exchangeable, usable value in religion seems to be what it reveals about human psychology, or what it does for social assimilation, or how it explains cultural conflict. Mentoring relationships, therefore, are very "un-modern." Mentors don't reduce things to the lowest common denominator. They don't filter spirituality to refine religion into what is "usable" to achieve mere contentment.

Mentoring is counter-cultural. It contradicts the trends of modern living, or the "dumbing," "numbing," and "slumming" tendencies of western culture.

The "dumbing" tendency of modern western culture is our predisposition to limit truth to that narrow band of facts that can be objectively verified. It doesn't matter what the question is that burdens our minds, tugs on our hearts, or dogs our footsteps. The answer must always be something like "3.14159," or the ratio of any human being's psychological state to the diameter of any human being's sociological context. In other words, life is a matter of sound geometry, and the key to the good life will always be the right equation, weight loss program, investment portfolio, personality mix, or career move.

If you had a church upbringing, consider how the worship service has evolved since the modern era emerged sometime in the early 18th century. At first, church members could easily cope with a 60 minute sermon, making multiple points, surrounded by a complex liturgical year. By the beginning of the 20th century, church members could only absorb a twenty minute sermon, making three points, and surrounded by the same liturgy repeated every week. By 1970 that had been reduced to a 15 minute sermon, making one point, accompanied by one of 15 favorite hymns. Today, church members can only cope with a 10 minute sermon, with a great story or memorable joke, accompanied by a cute children's time, and lots of coffee.

When mentors present *seven* experiences of grace, *seven* acts of mercy, *seven* lively virtues and deadly sins, and *seven* stages for spiritual growth, modern people complain. We can't memorize seven things, and believe it to be needlessly complicated and morally unfair if we're forced to do it. That is the "dumbing" tendency in modern western culture.

The "numbing" tendency of modern western culture is our predisposition to focus on ourselves, and to only expand our attention outward as time, talent, and money permit. We insulate ourselves from the rest of the world, and wrap ourselves in a cocoon of happiness of our own making, so that the problems and crises of others have less impact on our consciousness. We become "numb" to the world. We see it and use it, but try not to *feel it*.

If you had a church upbringing, consider how outreach has evolved since the modern era began. In the 19th century, local and global mission thrived. Mission Societies were fitting out special trains to the wild west, circuit riders were starting class meetings everywhere, and congregations were praying and paying for their own missionaries. By the late 1940's, mission deployment and capital pooling had centralized to the denomination, and churches had refocused toward membership assimilation and pastoral care in the emerging baby boom. Charity was definitely beginning at home. Giving to benevolence funds in churches peaked around the year 1965, and has remained on that plateau for almost 50 years — despite dramatic increases in budgets for property and personnel.

When mentors emphasize self-examination and cross-examination for personal mission and hands-on social service, modern people complain that that's what we pay clergy to do, or that, through percentage giving, we pay experts to do mission for us. At best, outreach is "second mile giving," and we never seem to get far enough ahead in financial stability and personal comfort to complete the first mile. That is the "numbing" tendency in modern western culture.

The "slumming" tendency in modern western culture is our predisposition to self-gratification. The goal of labor is not productivity, but vacation. The goal of financial planning is not service, but retirement. We are constantly looking for the short cut, the acceptable mediocrity, and the easy way out. Technology has made life more pleasant and less labor intensive. In 1950 sociologists and municipal planners were predicting a new "leisure" society, and by the new millennium people felt cheated that it hadn't arrived. Substance abuse and entertainment industries are booming, especially in a bad economy. Escape from reality is the new "normal" — the lifestyle that the wealthy model and to which the poor aspire.

If you had a church upbringing, consider how membership expectations have evolved since the modern era began. In the 19th century, utopian ideals thrived. Liberal arts universities and utopian communities were founded across America. Christian spirituality was demonstrated by constant church attendance. Members were expected to observe the sacraments regularly, follow private and family devotions, read the Bible, pray for strangers, and tithe. In the early 20th century, revivals and large Sunday Schools for adult education emerged. But by the close of the 20th century, only a fraction of those who considered themselves "spiritual persons" believed worship attendance to be important. Amateur sports, weekend barbecues, Sunday brunches, and "private time" were pursued religiously.

When mentors emphasize discipline for personal growth, modern people complain. When it comes to spiritual, physical, mental, or emotional fitness, they prefer overeating, sloppy dressing, casual relationships, limited vocabulary, guaranteed incomes, easy spirituality, and the unquestioned freedom to live selfishly. This is the "slumming" tendency in modern western culture.

It is easy for such a critique to turn into a rant — or worse, a sermon. The analyses of changes in western culture is complex. On the one hand, there is an acceleration of interest in spiritual things. On the other hand, there are dramatic declines in the credibility of religious institutions like the church. Both occur simultaneously in a context of comparative wealth and opportunity. Most people yearn to get close to God, and to create a just society, but hesitate to make the personal sacrifices and invest the time and energy to do it. After all, getting to the City of God may not happen in my lifetime … and it may require a lifetime of effort to even get close. Can't somebody invent a better helicopter to get us there? Can't God send an angel to bring the City of God here?

The mentoring relationship is the fresh alternative that an increasing minority of people chooses as a way to exercise their spiritual yearning. The mentor is not a helicopter pilot promising shortcuts to an audience with God, nor is the mentor an angel promising to deliver the fullness of God to your home or hospital bed tomorrow. We have discovered that neither institution nor self-help products will bring us to unity with God, or bring justice to our lives. We need *a relationship*. We need a relationship with someone who has gone further than we have, and who has had the compassion to turn back and help us catch up. The mentor doesn't need to be wise ... just wiser than us. The mentor doesn't need to be perfect ... just more attuned to perfection than us. The mentor can still be a seeker. Indeed, the mentor *had better be a seeker as well*, or he or she won't be much good as a mentor. The question is: *Are you that mentor?*

So you have second thoughts. If I respond to the call to be a mentor for others, will people think me arrogant? Will they immediately point out all my many faults? Will they laugh? Will they mock? If I respond to the call to be a mentor for others, will my family think me negligent? Will they complain? Will my spouse sue for divorce? Will my children feel unloved? And if I respond to the call to be a mentor, will I personally wrestle with my own inadequacies? Will I sometimes accuse myself of being a hypocrite? Will I find myself over my head and out of my depth? Will I tremble with fear, knowing that another human being is staking his or her lifestyle on my advice?

All of these are real possibilities. These second thoughts are what drive the mentor to become an even more ardent seeker. After all, no one would dare to be a mentor to a seeker unless both parties were surrounded by the Holy Spirit. The mentoring relationship would simply be too daunting, and would provoke overwhelming anxiety, unless the mentor truly believed that he or she was caught up in the greater mentoring of God. It is this that separates mentoring from the training, coaching, counseling, and teaching through which modernity nurtures her children. You can train, coach, counsel, and teach without any conviction of God, or any consciousness of God's real presence. But you can't live in that spiritual void *and mentor.*

Mentors all have different strengths and weaknesses. You may be stronger ... or weaker ... in the skills of training, coaching, counseling, and teaching. You bring what talents you have to the greater challenge of mentoring, and you learn new skills as needed. What make you a mentor are three aspirations:

✓ **Christ Centeredness**

Mentors have experience in grace. They have experienced gratuitous evil, but also unexplainable good. They have experienced the nearness of God, peeked through the portals of existence and sensed the infinite beyond, felt God's breath over their shoulders in difficult times, and momentarily recognized God incognito on the highway.

The experience of "Christ now" comprises the center of meaning around which the mentor's life revolves. While others are chasing success, accumulating wealth, or satisfying their desires, mentors make decisions and shape lives around the Good, the Beautiful, and the True. The perfect expression of incarnation is Christ, and it is living in the real presence of Christ that gives the mentor something to share.

✓ **Mission Mindedness**

Mentors have experience in service. They have experienced the indifference and intolerance of society, but also the love and acceptance of others. They have participated in the work of compassion. They have reached out to strangers, outsiders, foreigners, people in need who know it, people in need who don't realize it, and even enemies. They have felt rejection, but seen success.

The experience of "justice happening" is the motivation that drives them forward. They want blessing to happen again and again, until everyone is touched by hope. While others are prioritizing time with their families, caring for themselves, and generally minding their own business, mentors are minding God's business. They are participating in the greater mission to redeem the world.

✓ **Spiritual Discipline**

Mentors have experience in accountability. They have experienced failure and shame, but also repentance and reform. They have crafted disciplined lives that both fit and challenge their unique lifestyles. They pay attention, work hard, subdue their impulses to selfishness, exercise the muscles of their hearts, and explore the depths of their souls.

The experience of "soul searching" is the habit of daily living, but also the expectation of life after death. God holds mentors accountable, and God *will* hold them accountable. There is a daily reckoning, and there is an eternal reckoning. Mentors believe that a human being will not go blithely into heaven without undergoing a complete review of their additions to, or subtractions from, God's purpose of redemption. Spiritual discipline is the act of holding ourselves accountable for the gifts, opportunities, and relationships that were entrusted to us through baptism.

These are "aspirations." They are imperfectly achieved, but that does not let us off the hook. One "aspires" to them, but the connotations of being an "aspirant" suggests an earnestness that knows no bounds. The mentor is a seeker who has grown up. He or she has matured far beyond wishful thinking, vague idealism, and dreaming innocence. Mentors "breathe in" God's presence and "breathe out" God's purpose. (To breathe is to *aspirate*.) Mentors *ascend,* or mount, the spiritual incline toward paradise.[20] Truly, the heart of the mentor is restless until it rests in God.

Are you still having second thoughts? Does the journey toward Christian maturity, and the double-sidedness of "seeking" and "mentoring" both excite and alarm you? The seeds of skepticism have been sown very deeply in the human spirit by the decades of modernity. Is God just a romantic notion, historic superstition, psychological dependency, or sociological phenomenon? Is God's purpose of redemption, or the reunion of the infinite and the finite, just a philosophical abstraction, or does it weave through history in visible and mysterious ways? These are not just interesting questions that we might ponder when we have extra time. They reveal a more fundamental question, the answer to which determines how we live our lives today, tomorrow, and all the way through the aging process to the moment of death.

Am I created ... or am I coincidence? Modernity wants us to believe the latter. My life is not really *significant* beyond the few people who appreciate my presence, and even they will get over it. In the modern world, one's life *does not signify.* Lives can be terminated at random in the movies, or at random in a terrorist attack, and while some may grieve and others may rage, within a few short years nobody will care or even remember. *Is that how it really is? Is the human being fundamentally of no real consequence?* If not, then accountability is temporarily useful to coordinate peaceful co-existence, but easily sacrificed for self-advancement. Spiritual discipline ... indeed, any kind of discipline ... has little purpose beyond assuaging one's conscience and prolonging one's time span. Good

---

[20] This metaphor is best known through Dante Alighieri's *The Divine Comedy* (New York: Alfred A. Knopf, Everyman's Library, 1995). I describe the loss and redemption of the credibility of clergy using Dante's stages of purgatorio, inferno, and paradiso in my book *Why Should I Believe You?* (Nashville: Abingdon Press, 2008).

luck is probably more important. In such a modern world, we need coaches, teachers, counselors, and trainers … but not mentors.

Mentors believe people are created. They are designed. They come from, and go to. Each individual's contribution to a larger purpose may be small, but it is of consequence. Life *signifies* something, although that "something" may be mysterious. *How you live* matters more than just "putting in time," "getting by," or even "living happily." Therefore, accountability is bigger than any individual's conscience, or any society's rules. Seekers become mentors when they are prepared endure pain, believe *in spite of* doubt, and even shorten their life spans in order to live and die well. Mentors believe that lives have significance beyond existence, and that it is that significance which makes existence itself valuable, beautiful, and purposeful.

If you believe people are created, then set aside your second thoughts. You have taken your first step as a seeker, and already you are capable of mentoring the vast majority of modern skeptics. Every step you take as a seeker opens the possibility for you to mentor those who come after you. The goal of mentoring is to multiply more mentors. The promise is passed on from each mentor to each seeker, and from each pilgrim to each traveling companion: *Seek and you will find.*